BAe 146

MODERN CIVIL AIRCRAFT:11

BAe 146

M.J.Hardy

LONDON

IAN ALLAN LTD

Contents

First published 1991

ISBN 0 7110 2010 8

Published by Ian Allan Ltd, Shepperton, Surrey; and printed by Ian Allan Printing Ltd at their works at Coombelands in Runnymede, England

Photo Acknowledgements
Unless otherwise stated, all the photographs in this book have been provided by British Aerospace (Commercial Aircraft) Ltd, and the author's grateful thanks are due to its Chief Public Relations Photographer, Darryl Cott, for his assistance in providing the illustrations; and also to Mike Gradidge and Olivier Constant for their help with photographs.
M.J.H.

Introduction

For quite a long time in its early career, the BAe146 seemed to be the airliner that nobody wanted, powered by American engines that were a second-best choice. The Hawker Siddeley. HS146 project, on which work started in April 1971, was preceded by a decade of independent design studies by de Havilland and Hawker Siddeley for a short-haul jet, all of which came to nothing because of the lack of a suitable powerplant for this category of airliner. This quest for such an engine was certainly not helped by the succession of mergers that occurred in the British aircraft and aero-engine industries in the early 1960s. These led to the demise not only of the de Havilland Engine Co, with its unrivalled tradition of expertise in small engines going back to the Gipsy and Gipsy Major of prewar days, but also of Bristol Aero-Engines, Armstrong-Siddeley, Blackburn and Napier, all of which had a strong affinity with small engines. This would have provided an ideal background for the development of British equivalents of the well-known Pratt & Whitney Canada PT6 or Garrett TPE331 turboprops, as well as small turbofans suitable for short-haul jets of which the HS146 was one.

But 'Big was Beautiful' in official thinking, and corporatism 'ruled OK' throughout the 1960s and most of the 1970s. The bankruptcy of Rolls-Royce in 1970 and the need to secure the development of the big RB211 turbofan led to the axeing of some smaller civil engine projects. The RB172 turbofan, which might well have powered the 146 after the RB203 Trent's earlier demise, was earmarked, in its developed form as the RT172/T.260 Adour, to power the SEPECAT Jaguar and later the Hawker Siddeley Hawk. This left the Avco Lycoming ALF 502 turbofan as the best — indeed almost the only — choice for the HS146 project, which finally received the go-ahead in August 1973. The 146 became the first British airliner to go into production without British engines, even as an optional choice for the customer, yet it remains the only airliner to be powered by the ALF 502.

The choice of engine was the first major hurdle surmounted by the 146 but, once started, it faced a turbulent political and economic scene. The fuel price rises following the Arab-Israeli Yom Kippur war of October 1973 were leading to a worldwide recession, while at home inflation was rising, reaching 17 per cent in August 1974.

Above:
Air UK's first 146 Series 200, G-CNMF, is seen here in its Class B test registration G-5-079 and flew the airline's first 146 service, from Guernsey to London-Heathrow on 14 December 1987. *Fleet PR*

Previous page:
The second 146 Series 100, G-SSHH, in flight.
All photographs are copyright of BAe unless stated otherwise.

Above:
The 146 Series 300 prototype, G-LUXE, converted to this form from the first 146, G-SSSH.

An increasingly militant trade union movement led to the Tories fighting and losing two elections in February and October that year on a 'Who Rules Britain?' ticket. And Labour's victories in both cases, together with their pledge to nationalise the aircraft industry, did not make for confidence in planning projects like the HS146. Neither did the electioneering atmosphere that prevailed throughout 1974 and, with the world's scheduled airlines facing sizeable losses, Hawker Siddeley decided in October that year that the HS146 project was no longer commercially viable.

Work on the 146 ceased, while strenuous trade union efforts were made to save it. Without any firm orders to its name, the 146 might so easily have suffered the fate of many other British projects — cancellation. Instead it was 'put on ice' for what was to be nearly four years, design and research continuing on a limited basis to be ready for future relaunching. Only about 75 people were working on the 146 project in the first year after the programme was halted, this figure rising to 250 in the year before the project was relaunched as the BAe146 in July 1978. The bill nationalising the aircraft industry and creating British Aerospace (BAe) had received Royal assent in March 1977, and the 146 became the new state enterprise's civil flagship. The launch customer (after the first order from Argentina had lapsed) was not to be a British airline, but Air Wisconsin, which placed its first order in May 1981, nearly three years after the relaunch. The 146 has proved especially popular among the US regional or commuter airlines, due not least to its exceptional quietness which has enabled it to operate out of airports like Burbank, San Jose and Orange County's John Wayne in California, which serve highly noise-sensitive communities. The ALF 502, initially regarded as rather a second-best choice, has made the 146 the World's quietest airliner.

Other notable export orders were from China's state airline CAAC and those very demanding buyers, the Ansett airlines, in Australia and New Zealand. Sales received a considerable boost when the Australian TNT Group committed itself in June 1987 to buying all the 146-QT freighters to be built in the next five years, a total of 72 aircraft (of which firm orders for 23 have so far been placed, for operation by a number of European freight carriers under contract to TNT. The countries of eastern Europe, now turning to market economies after years of Communist rule, are likely to buy the 146 and BAe has already had talks with Poland's state airline LOT about the purchase of 146s. Above all, the 146's exceptional quietness accords so well with today's concern for the environment and the quality of life.

M. J. Hardy,
Selsey, West Sussex

1 Design Origins

By the beginning of the 1970s, the concept of the short-haul jet pioneered by the BAC One-Eleven was well and truly established. The British jet had inaugurated the world's first short-haul jet service on 9 April 1965 when a One-Eleven 201 of British United Airways had flown from London to Genoa. The One-Eleven had been followed into service by the Douglas DC-9, which began revenue-earning flights with Delta Air Lines of Atlanta, Georgia, on 8 December 1965, and by the Boeing 737, with which Lufthansa started services on 10 February 1968 and United Air Lines on 28 April that year. By 1970, when over 200 had been sold, the One-Eleven as earning more foreign exchange than any other British civil aircraft then being exported, and had become Britain's biggest ever individual dollar earner, even against a 10% US tariff barrier. Moreover, by that year One-Eleven production costs for some time had been sufficiently low to achieve a healthy profit margin on each aircraft built, and this was making a significant contribution to paying off launch and development costs. Clearly the One-Eleven programme provided a firm basis on which to build future British airliner success stories, but for various reasons — in particular the Rolls-Royce bankruptcy of 1970 and the Arab-Israeli Yom Kippur war of 1973 with its associated fuel price rises and recessionary effect on world trade — this proved to be more difficult than might have been expected a few years earlier.

Indeed, the British Aerospace BAe146, which was to succeed the One-Eleven as our most important civil airliner export, had a somewhat prolonged gestation period that reflected the political uncertainties of the mid-1970s as much as any technical problems.

As related later, the BAe146 programme was temporarily halted in October 1974 for nearly four years, largely because of the recession and fuel price rises that followed on the Yom Kippur war of 1973, design and research continuing on a limited basis. The BAe146's origins go back to 1959-60 when both de Havilland and Hawker Siddeley — then of course, both still separate

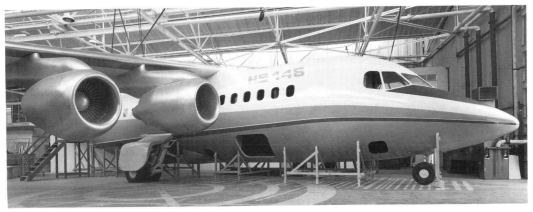

Above:
The full-scale wooden mock-up of the HS146 (later to be BAe146) at Hatfield early in 1974, with Boeing 747 seats in the passenger cabin.

Right:
The first 146 Series 100, G-SSSH, at the rollout ceremony at Hatfield on 20 May 1981. In the foreground are the flags of Sweden, the UK and the USA, the three nations participating in the 146 programme.

groups — were studying various airliner projects to replace the widely-used Douglas DC-3.

Many thousands of this well-loved workhorse had become available at the end of hostilities at cheap war-surplus prices, and with its low initial and operating costs, and ability to operate from small unprepared airfields, it had become the most widely-used airliner in the world. There was hardly an air force in the world that did not have at least some in its inventory. In 1945-46 it was being confidently predicted that the DC-3 would be replaced by about 1950, at least on the major inter-city routes, but 10 years after the war there were still some 1,650 of them in airline service, and the type equipped no less than 46 different air forces. Several airlines modified their DC-3s to their own ideas to improve payload and performance, producing variants like BEA's 'Pionair'-class Dakotas and Pan Am's HI-per DC-3. As late as 1974, one US company was proposing a re-engined DC-3 variant known as the Super Turbo Three with two Rolls-Royce Dart turboprops, and this was succeeded three years later by the Tri Turbo-3, a re-engined DC-3 with three 850shp Pratt & Whitney PT6A-41 turboprops, one in each wing nacelle and one in the nose.

The sheer size of the DC-3 replacement market was in one sense illusory, because the type was replaced by many different types for different categories of operation; by Convair 240s and S40s and Martin 4-0-4s; later by Viscounts and Friendships, and later still by jets on the major inter-city routes: by de Havilland Herons or Twin Otters and later still by turboprops such as the Jetstream, Bandeirante or Metro on third level or commuter-type routes and for rural air services, so that no one type of aircraft could really lay claim to the title of the definitive DC-3 replacement. Nor would putting the type back into production after the war in its original form have solved the problem, as the DC-3 would not have complied with current airworthiness requirements.

De Havilland Projects

It was not surprising that de Havilland at Hatfield, with a long tradition going back to prewar days of providing aircraft for the smaller airline serving the less populous or more isolated communities, with types such as the Dragon Rapide, Dove and Heron, should have had a go at the DC-3 replacement challenge of 1959. This was a twin-engined high wing design seating 32-40 passengers, and powered by two 1,150shp Gnome turboprops; Bristol Aero-Engines had acquired the licence to build the T58 Gnome from General Electric, and the first Bristol-built Gnome had made its first test run on 5 June 1959. The DH123, with a span of 81ft 3in, a length overall of 60ft 6in and a maximum take-off weight of 22,100lb, compared very closely in terms of size and horsepower with France's Nord 262, and the project was presented as a 'branchliner' at the 1959 SBAC Show at Farnborough.

However, in January 1960 de Havilland was taken over by Hawker Siddeley, becoming the de Havilland Division of the Hawker Siddeley Group, as part of the Duncan Sandys-inspired rationalisation of the aircraft industry. The DH 123 was now in direct competition with another Hawker Siddeley Group aircraft, the rather larger 36-44 passenger Avro 748 with two Rolls-Royce Darts, for which the Hawker Siddeley board had given the go-ahead in January 1959. The first prototype Avro 748 made its maiden flight on 24 June 1960, and Skyways Coach Air was the first to put the type into service in 1962, followed by Aerolineas Argentinas.

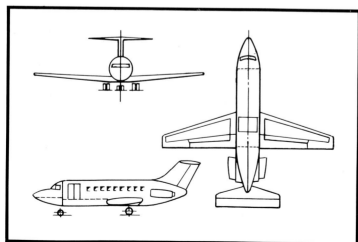

The DH126 of 1960

De Havilland Short-Haul Jet Projects 1959-64

	DH123	DH126	DH126	DH126	DH126
Date	1959	Mid-1960	April 1961	End 1963	February 1964
Engines	2 x 1,150shp Gnome turbo-props	2 x 3,850lb st DH PS92 (or PS92B)	2 x 4,050lb st Rolls-Royce RB172-3 turbofans	2 x 4,200lb st GE CF700-2B turbofans	2 x 4,600lb st Rolls-Royce RB172
Passengers	32-40	30	32	26-32	26-32
Span	81ft 0in	62ft 0in	62ft 0in	67ft 0in	67ft 0in
Length	60ft 6in	60ft 3in	60ft 3in	62ft 8in	62ft 8in
Wing Area	550sq ft	550sq ft	550sq ft	600sq ft	600sq ft
Max Take-off Weight	22,100lb	22,500lb	23,600lb	28,000lb	29,250lb

The DH 123 was accordingly dropped, both because it conflicted with the Avro 748 and also because technical opinion at Hatfield still favoured the jet over the turboprop, even for short-haul stages, because of its superior passenger appeal. A 40-passenger project with two 5,700lb st Rolls-Royce RB145s was briefly studied, but Hatfield's next attempt was the DH 126 of mid-1960, a low wing design resembling a slightly larger DH125 executive jet and with a cabin size matched as closely as possible to the DC-3. It would have had two rear-mounted turbojets like the DH125 and, initially, these would have been de Havilland PS92 (and PS92B) engines of 3,850lb st. (This powerplant was not built because the de Havilland Engine Co was acquired by Bristol Siddeley Engines Ltd in November 1961).

The DH126 was then studied with two 4,050lb st Rolls-Royce RB172-3 turbofans, and with this and the earlier PS92 engines it would have had a span of 62ft 0in, a length of 60ft 3in, and seating for 26-32 passengers. Maximum take-off weight would have been 23,600lb with RB172-3 engines. The DH126 was designed specifically to operate over very short stage lengths, and from field lengths as small as 3,300ft. Because of this, the project attracted a good deal of interest, especially among the Australian domestic airlines to whom a presentation was made. Later, at the end of 1963, two 4,200lb st General Electric CF700-2B turbo fans were considered as alternative powerplants, followed early in 1964 by a more powerful variant of the RB172 rated at 4,600lb st. With these two powerplants, wingspan

was increased by 5ft and length grew to 62ft 8in, maximum take-off weight with the CF700-2Bs being 28,000lb.

The DH126 compared pretty closely with the 28-32 passenger seating and maximum take-off weight of 25,200 to 28,000lb of most Douglas DC-3s in service at that time. But none of the three types of jet engine envisaged for the DH126 was either available or of proven suitability for commercial use. Like every other manufacturer studying short-haul jet projects at this time — including its rivals Hunting Aircraft Ltd, whose H107 jet airliner project was taken over by BAC and developed into the One-Eleven — de Havilland had to face the problem that the choice of jet engines for a genuinely short-haul project was severely limited. Nor were matters helped by the succession of mergers that occurred in the British aircraft and aero-engine industry in the early 1960s, which led to the extinction not only of the de Havilland Engine Co, the natural source for a powerplant for a DH jet project, but also to such smaller engine firms as Armstrong-Siddeley Motors Ltd and Blackburn Engines Ltd, which became part of Bristol Siddeley, and also D. Napier & Son Ltd, makers of the Eland turboprop.

All of these firms had a particular affinity for the smaller type of engine which went back to prewar days with such powerplants as the Armstrong Siddeley Lynx, Jaguar and Cheetah radials, the DH Gipsy, Gipsy Major and Gipsy Six and the Blackburn Cirrus Minor in-line engines, as well as the Napier Lion. All this would have provided a wealth of experience that could have gone into British equivalents of the well known Pratt & Whitney Canada PT6 or Garret TPE331 turboprops, as well as commercial turbofans in the lower power brackets. But in the early 1990s we have the melancholy situation in which not one British airliner currently in production is available with British engines, even as an alternative optional choice for the customer. It can certainly be argued that this is due to the over-contraction of our aero-engine industry that took place in the early 1960s, as well as the priority that had to be given to first saving, and then ensuring, the development of the big RB211 turbofan after the Rolls-Royce bankruptcy of 1970.

A factor basic to all short-haul jet airliner project studies at this time was the virtual impossibility of designing a new small aircraft with operating costs per seat-mile better than an older, larger and written-down type such as a DC-3 or Convair 340/440. They could also usually offer equal costs per aircraft mile and this was especially true if the new airliner had new and untried turbofan engines — its operating economics could not have stood comparison with older, written-down types. An added factor was the emergence of re-engining programmes in which existing piston-engined airliners, such as the Convairliner, were fitted with turboprops; this had been pioneered by Napier, which first flew as Convair 340 powered by Nel.1 Eland turboprops in February 1955, this version serving in small numbers with Allegheny Airlines Inc and the Royal Canadian Air Force. This was followed by the Convair 580, a Convair 340 or 440 fitted with Allison 501-D13 turboprops, of which 130 were produced, all but 20 for airline use, especially by local service carriers Frontier, Allegheny and Lake Central in the United States. There was also the Rolls-Royce Dart-powered Convair 600 and 640 conversions of the Models 240, 340 and 440 of which nearly 70 were produced.

Hawker Siddeley Projects
However, the de Havilland team at Hatfield had continued to hold faith in the small twin-turbofan airliner as the right DC-3 replacement. It believed not only that a twin turboprop would compete too directly with the Hawker Siddeley 748 (as the Avro 748 was now known) and the Fokker/Fairchild Friendship, as well as with the turboprop Convairs, but also that any turboprop-powered design would be an interim step of relatively limited life. Short-haul jet design studies continued at Hatfield after de Havilland's takeover under Hawker Siddeley, which continued the old de Havilland sequence of type numbers, so that the HS131 was the next short-haul jet project after the DH126. In an effort to minimise development costs, the HS131 of 1963-64 was meant to embody as many Hawker Siddeley 748 components as possible in a low-wing rear-engined layout powered by two 5,000lb st Rolls-Royce RB172 turbofans, and seating 28-32 passengers. The 748 front fuselage, flightdeck, cabin furnishings and many of the systems, were found suitable for

Hawker Siddeley Jet Projects Preceding The 146

	HS131	HS136	HS136	HS136-100	HS136-200	HS 144-100	HS144-200
Date	1964	1964	1967	End 1968	End 1968	1969	1969
Engines	2 x 5,000lb st Rolls-Royce RB172	2 x 6,000lb st Rolls-Royce RB172-57	2 x 9,730lb st Rolls-Royce RB203 Trent under wings	2 x 9,730lb st RB203 Trent	2 x 9,730lb st RB203 Trent	2 x 10,640lb st RB203-Trent	2 x 10,640lb st RB203-12 Trent
Passengers	28-32	36-40	50-57	60-79	70-93	53-62	70-80
Span	67ft 0in	64ft 9in	83ft 6in	90ft 6in	90ft 6in	83ft 4in	83ft 4in
Length	62ft 8in	70ft 4in	72ft 0in	76ft 6in	82ft 8in	86ft 5in	96ft 3in
Wing Area	640sq ft	600sq ft	800sq ft			767sq ft	767sq ft
Max Take-off Weight	30,000lb	34,000lb	54,000lb	59,850lb		57,200lb	64,100lb

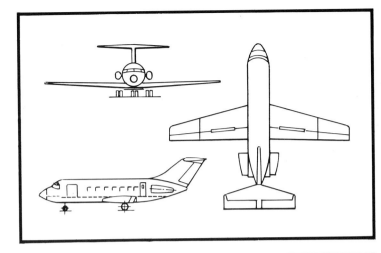

The HS131 of 1964

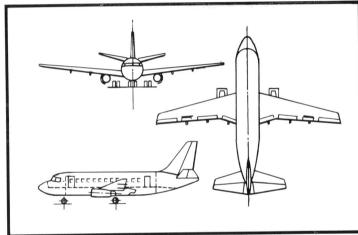

The HS136 of 1967

incorporation into the HS131, but it still needed an entirely new wing, undercarriage and tail unit so that the saving in using some 748 components was not all that great, and the degree of commonality with the 748 would have been fairly limited. Wingspan would have been 67ft 0in and length 62ft 8in (the same as the later DH126) and maximum take-off weight would have been 30,000lb. Also studied as possible powerplants were the Bristol Siddeley BS304 and General Electric CF700 turbofans; the latter, in its CF700-2B form, was at that time the only small turbofan likely to be available, powering France's Dassault Mystere 20 executive jet, but its maximum take-off thrust of 4,200lb was really too low for projects like the DH126 and HS131.

Finding a suitable engine that was likely to be available and in production still remained the problem, and in mid-1964 another series of studies of a low-wing rear-engined layout was started under the designation HS136. This was initially a 36-40 passenger aircraft with two 6,000lb st Rolls-Royce RB172-57s and a maximum take-off weight of 34,000lb. Wingspan was 64ft 9in, length 70ft 4in and wing area 600sq ft, and like the HS131 and DH126 before it, a T-tail was featured to keep the tailplane clear of jet efflux. Two years later the project had grown into a four-abreast 50-seater and by early 1967 into a five-abreast 57-seater. This last stage was accompanied by an all-round increase in size and power, no doubt partly influenced by the growing BAC One-Eleven order book and the use made of this type by important carriers like Braniff International and Mohawk Airlines on multi-stop local service-type routes previously operated by Convairs, and not so many years before by DC-3s. The HS136 in its enlarged form was powered by two 9,730lb st Rolls-Royce RB203 Trent turbofans, an engine developed as a low specific fuel consumption successor to the Spey for short-haul transports in the 1970s. The Trent, which first ran in December 1967, was the first Rolls-Royce three-shaft engine to be run; the

RB172 studied for previous projects was now being developed jointly with Turbomeca of France as the RB172/T260 Adour to power the BAC-Breguet Jaguar. The Trent was in fact initially developed for Fairchild's FH-228 licence-built version of the Fokker F28 Fellowship, but in 1968 Fairchild decided to drop its plans to build this version.

A major configurational revision accompanied the change to Trents for the HS136, these engines now being mounted under the wings like the Boeing 737 instead of on the rear fuselage. The advantages claimed for this arrangement were the elimination of deep stall and engine flame-out problems that had troubled the One-Eleven, improved engine accessibility, better flexibility of passenger loading and ease of future fuselage 'stretches'. Against this was the greater likelihood of intake ingestion causing damage to the engine, especially when operating from unprepared surfaces, because of the greater proximity of the intake lip to the ground. But tests on the Hawker Siddeley HS125 executive jet were to show that with this engine position, the danger of debris ingestion was very real, and so the next short-haul jet project, the HS144, reverted to a rear-mounted position.

With Trents, the HS136 now had a wingspan of 83ft 6in, a length of 72ft 0in, a wing area of 800sq ft and a maximum take-off weight of 54,000lb. It was now very close, in terms of size, power and payload, to what the BAC 107 (formerly Hunting H107) had been in September 1960 just before it had been re-engined with two 9,850lb st Rolls-Royce RB163 Speys, to become the BAC One-Eleven; and the break from the 26-32 seats of previous de Havilliand and Hawker Siddeley projects to 50 and more seats showed that the impossibility of achieving acceptable economics in a new jet, seating the same number of passengers as a DC-3, was now fully realised.

At the end of 1968 two further HS136 variants were studied, both with Trent turbofans. These were the 60-79 passenger HS136-100, and the 70-93 passenger HS136-200, both of which had

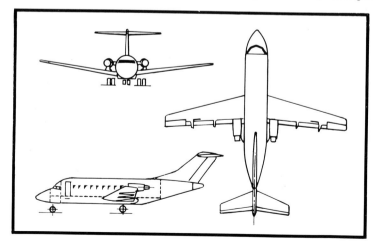

The HS144 of 1969

12

a 7ft increase in wingspan. Length of the 136-100 was 76ft 6in, while that of the -200 was 82ft 8in. The 136-200 was now practically the same size as that of the BAC One-Eleven 200 on its launch in May 1961, and the BAC jet would have had the advantage of an earlier start over the HS136 had the latter gone into production, while the 136 would also have been up against the 60-passenger Fokker F28 Fellowship with two 9,250lb st RB183-2 Spey Junior turbofans.

There was also domestic competition with the Hawker Siddeley Group itself, because at Manchester the Avro Whitworth Division had been engaged in studies of turbojet and turbofan developments of the basic Avro 748, of which over 170 had been sold by late 1967. The HS860 project was basically a 748 with two Trent turbofans mounted on the rear fuselage, with the wing, fuselage and tail unit being extensively modified to cater for the change to jet propulsion. Airline reaction to this had been described as 'encouraging' by Hawker Siddeley's marketing department in Manchester, but the main Hawker Siddeley board called for a comparative evaluation of the HS860 and HS136 to help decide which of the two should get the go-ahead. In the end the board decreed that project work should continue on the basis of a completely new design, and so both the Manchester and Hatfield teams began working together to produce a joint final design.

This led in mid-1969 to the HS144 project, which reverted to a rear-mounted position for its two 10,640lb st RB203-12 Trent turbofans, because of possible ingestion problems with engines mounted under the wing. The tailplane, which had been low-set on the HS136, reverted to the top of the fin. The extreme rear of the fuselage opened to form two petal-type air brakes, a feature which was incorporated into the BAe146. To improve the centre of gravity distribution, the engines were mounted much further forward than might have been expected — over the wing trailing edge, in fact — and there was, rather unusually, a passenger entrance door aft of the engines instead of ventral airstairs as on the One-Eleven or a forward entrance door as on the Fellowship. There were two basic variants of the project, the 53-62 passenger HS144-100 with a length of 86ft 5in and maximum take-off weight of 57,200lb, and the 70-80 passenger HS144-200, with a length of 96ft 3in and maximum gross weight of 64,100lb. Both variants had a wing area of 767sq ft and 83ft 4in span, and compared pretty closely to the Fokker F26 Fellowship in terms of size and payload.

However, in 1968 Fairchild abandoned its plans to build the Fellowship under licence as the FH-228 powered by two RB203 Trents and, as a result of this decision, work on Trent development slowed down and stopped completely after the Rolls-Royce financial collapse of 1970. Once again, a short-haul jet project had been defeated by the lack of a suitable engine, and this difficulty in finding a suitable powerplant would surely not have occurred if the de Havilland Engine Co and Bristol Aero-Engines had still been in existence as separate entities. Rolls-Royce's Bristol Engine Division (as Bristol Aero-Engines had now become) was now fully preoccupied with development of the Olympus 593 for Concorde and the Pegasus for the Harrier, as well as participating in the Rolls-Royce RB199 development for the Tornado and the M45H turbofan for the German VFW 614 short-haul airliner.

While more conventional short-haul projects like the HS136 and HS144 were being studied, Hawker-Siddeley was beginning to get deeply involved in the A300 Airbus, starting with the HBN 100 project revealed in March 1966. This was a 261-passenger joint Hawker Siddeley/Breguet/Nord design with two Pratt & Whitney JT9D-1 turbofans, and was a forerunner of the Airbus. When the British government withdrew from the Airbus consortium in March 1969 because of the absence of any firm orders at that time, Hawker-Siddeley remained as a full risk-sharing partner with responsibility of designing and building the wing, a position British Aerospace continues to occupy to this day.

Also studied in some detail for use in the mid-1980s was the HS141 fan-lift V/STOL project for around 100 to 120 passengers, which would have had no less than 16 Rolls-Royce RB202 fan lift engines and two RB220 turbofans in the 20,000lb st class for forward propulsion. These were to be mounted under the small, conventionally-swept wings, while the lift engines were housed in a long fairing under the fuselage. Since the RB202 lift engines would have produced about 10,000lb st each, it seems obvious today that noise, if no other consideration, would have put paid to this project for operations out of city centres. But a number of variants of the basic HS141 were studied, including specialised STOL versions with eight, six and four RB202 lift engines, some of these incorporating coupled tip-driven lift fans. Using VTOL like the Harrier, the HS141 would have had a range of just under 400 miles, which could have been increased by up to 800 miles using a short take-off from a 1,000ft field and long-range cruise techniques. Hawker-Siddeley also studied several RTOL (reduced take-off and landing) airliner projects for operation from close-in and regional airfields in the 1970s, including one such study based on the Trident medium-haul jet.

Meanwhile, with the demise of the Trent after the Rolls-Royce collapse, several other engines were studied as possibilities for powering the project that would succeed the HS144. These included the Rolls-Royce Spey, RB410 and RB415; the General Electric TF34 which was designed to power the Lockheed S-3A Viking anti-submarine aircraft; the M45 turbofan, that had been started as a joint venture by the French aero-engine company SNECMA and Bristol Siddeley Engines, the latter now being a wholly-owned subsidiary of Rolls-Royce; and another American turbofan, the Avco Lycoming 502. The first of the M45 series of turbofans, the M45F demonstrator, had made its initial test-run on 7 June 1966, and the M45H civil version had been designed especially to meet the low specific fuel consumption needs of the German VFW614 (later VFW-Fokker 614) short-haul 40-44-seat airliner, which was powered by two 7,280lb st M45Hs mounted one on a pylon above each wing. The VFW 614 first flew on 14 July 1971 but this German-Dutch collaborative venture was not a commercial success. This was due at least in part to the fact that it was too small for the short-haul jet market (as it was then developing), being up against Fokker's own F28 Fellowship, and being closer, in terms of size and payload, to the HS136 in its original form. So it was not surprising that the M45H turbofan was thought to be too expensive and too large for Hawker Siddeley's HS146 short-haul project that succeeded the HS144.

The HS146 Emerges

In the wake of the Rolls-Royce bankruptcy of 1970 and subsequent reorganisation, development of several civil aero engines was either terminated or did not proceed. The Trent, as mentioned earlier, was discontinued, and several uprated variants of the Spey, such as the Spey 67C, which would have powered the proposed stretched One-Eleven 600 and 700, did not go ahead.

The RB172 studied for the DH126 and HS131 was now, in its developed form as the RB172/T260 Adour, earmarked to power the Jaguar and later the Hawker Siddeley Hawk, while the RB410 and RB415 had not gone ahead. This left the Avco Lycoming ALF 502 turbofan as the best available choice for the HS146; the engine, was first run as a complete unit in June 1971 and had been launched in 1969, mainly as a powerplant for executive jets, the ALF 502L-2 powering the Canadair CL601 Challenger. It was a de-rated civil version of the 7,000lb st F102 military turbofan which had powered the Northrop A-9A, the losing entry in the US Air Forces's A-X close-support aircraft competition of 1970-72 which had been won by the Fairchild Republic A-10A Thunderbolt II. The F102 itself was closely related to the Lycoming T55 free-turbine turboshaft that was supplied in large numbers to power the Boeing Vertol CH-47 Chinook; by 1974 well over 2,000 T55s had been delivered, and total flying time with this engine was now in excess of 3 million hours, much of it in the hazardous and demanding conditions of Vietnam. The ALF 502 embodied the gas generator section (compressor, annular combustion chamber and turbine) of the T-55-L-11B variant as its core, this model powering the CH-47C Chinook and, in the process of refining the F102 for commercial use as the ALF 502, the basic design was modified to satisfy the commercial needs of long life and low-cost operation, with on-condition maintenance instead of a fixed TBO (Time Between Overhauls), although a TBO of 4,000hrs has been granted. Construction was made totally modular for ease of maintenance.

However, when work started on the HS146 project in April 1971, the modest thrust of only 6,500lb st of the ALF 502 chosen to power it, meant that four engines were necessary instead of the two of all the previous short-haul jet projects, if the HS146 was to carry its envisaged payload of 70 passengers and offer a range of 700 nautical miles. The intake ingestion problems that had been foreseen with the HS136's two Trents mounted under the wings like the Boeing 737, dictated a high shoulder-mounted wing with 3° anhedral at the trailing edge and 15° sweepback at the quarter chord line, under which the ALF 502s were mounted on pylons; wing area was initially 800sq ft, span was 84ft 10in and length 86ft 2in. Up to 88 passengers could be carried and maximum take-off weight was initially 70,000lb.

This four-engined layout did have the advantage of giving the HS146 a take-off field performance as good as twin turboprops like the

Herald and 748 which it was intended to replace, something that none of the previous jet projects studied had been able to achieve in the same degree. Market research had already shown that there was little, if any, demand for real STOL performance from prospective customers for this sort of jet, as hardly any potential operation really needed a field length of less than 3,000ft, and for perhaps 90 per cent of them a field length of 3,500ft or more would be satisfactory. This made it possible to dispense with the complexities of high-lift devices such as leading edge flaps. Fowler area-increasing flaps spanning 78 per cent of each wing trailing edge, working with three lift-dumpers on each wing upper surface that extend automatically on touchdown, enable short field lengths to be achieved.

Indeed, design philosophy of the 146 has very much aimed at keeping it simple; the type has no leading edge flaps, no thrust reversers, no composite materials in its construction, and engine hush kits are unnecessary (it was not until several years after design work started that the ALF 502's great quietness proved to be a major selling point for airlines serving noise-conscious communities, especially in the United States). The swept-back fixed incidence tailplane is mounted on top of the fin to ensure clearance from jet efflux and wing turbulence. The undercarriage features twin Dunlop wheels on each unit, the main wheels retracting inwards into blister-type fairings on the fuselage sides and the steerable nosewheel retracting forwards. The undercarriage track is actually wider than that of the Lockheed C-130 Hercules, and a generous fuselage diameter of 11ft 8in was chosen to provide 5-abreast seating as comfortable as that to be found in wide-body jets — an important point, since today's passenger expect (as far as possible) big jet standards of comfort in the short-haul jet they transfer to for a regional or commuter flight. Conventional light alloy

Above:
The typical six-abreast cabin interior of a Dan-Air 146 Series 100 seen here seats 86-88 passengers.

Right:
An ALF 502R-5 turbofan with cowlings open demonstrates the ease of accessibility for maintenance conferred by the underslung position. On-condition maintenance is usual with these engines, although a fixed TBO (Time Between Overhaul) of 4,000hr has been approved.

construction is used throughout the 146, and the maximum cabin pressure differential is 6.5lb/sq in.

Initially, the AL 502H of 6,700lb st and a by-pass ratio of 6:1 was the variant chosen to power the 146, and the engine in its military F102 form had first been flight-tested under a modified North American AJ-2 Savage twin-engined attack bomber in 1972. The engine is built up from four basic modules consisting of the fan, accessory gearbox, gas producer/compressor and combustion turbine, and it comprised the compressor, annular combustion chamber and turbine from the T55-L-11 turboshaft to which was added a gearbox, the single-stage front fan and an additional supercharger stage. All four engine pods on the 146 are interchangeable, despite differing equipment standards. Two basic variants of the aircraft were offered as definitive versions: the HS146-100 seating 70 passengers five-abreast or up to 88 six-abreast, with a length of 85ft 10in; and the stretched HS146-200, seating 82 five-abreast or up to 102 six-abreast, with a length of 93ft 1in. The span of both variants was now 86ft 6in. This was the form in which the 146 was offered to potential customers, and presented to the British government with a request for financial backing.

This request at first aroused some mixed feelings, for at that time, in 1973, international collaboration was de rigeur politically, and was exemplified in programmes such as the Airbus, Concorde, the Panavia MRCA (to become the Tornado) and Jaguar. But these were advanced technology projects — in the cases of Concorde and MRCA, on the very frontiers of technology, and with correspondingly high cost to match. The 146, by contrast, was a basically simple aeroplane, well within the capabilities of a major group like Hawker Siddeley without overstretching its resources, and to force such a project into an international collaborative framework would merely add extra layers of management and cost and perhaps lead to unsatisfactory compromises being built into the design. As the VFW-Fokker 614 and later Concorde itself were to show, large-scale commercial success did not necessarily follow because a programme involved more than one nation. The British aircraft industry badly needed a new civil project if its current high rate of aerospace exports was to be maintained in the 1980s, and the 146's basically simple design means that development costs were likely to be recovered that much quicker by a levy on sales.

Luckily, these arguments won the day and on 29 August 1973 Hawker Siddeley announced that it was to produce the HS146 with government support, which amounted to some £40 million at January 1972 prices (£46 million at August 1973 prices) with Hawker Siddeley investing a similar amount. The government's risk-sharing investment was to be recovered by a levy on sales extending for the life of the programme, Hawker Siddeley agreeing to bear any cost over-runs. Earlier that year, Hawker Siddeley had estimated that by 1982 there would be a market for some 1,500 aircraft in the 146 category, of which the 146's share could be at least 420. After 14 years of study of short-haul jet and turboprop projects, the 146 at last had the go-ahead, although there was some resentment in Dutch government circles, and in Germany too, at the competitive threat the 146 represented to the Fokker F28 Fellowship and also to the VFW-Fokker 614. But it was pointed out that the short-haul market was big enough for at least two types, and that no Common Market country was entitled to lay claim to a monopoly of any particular part of the airliner market.

2 The Project is Shelved

With the go-ahead given at last, work on the HS146 gathered momentum in the closing months of 1973 and early months of 1974, geared to a first flight scheduled for December 1975 and certification in February 1977. Initial plans called for production of two batches of six aircraft to be followed by subsequent batches of 10, and thereafter batches of increasing size. The seventh aircraft was to be the first Series 200, with a first flight scheduled for February 1977 and certification for the following August; initially it was expected that the Series 200 might account for some 30 per cent of sales. A full-scale wooden mock-up was built at Hatfield, with Boeing 747 seats in the passenger cabin for the benefit of prospective customers, and by April 1974, when the first metal was cut, work on the engineering mock-up was well advanced.

Overall design responsibility was vested at Hatfield, which was also where final assembly was to take place, and design and production work on the HS146 was apportioned between Hatfield, Manchester and Brough design offices. Thus, Manchester was to be responsible for the complete tail unit and rear fuselage, and the wing trailing edge structure and moving surfaces such as flaps; the former Blackburn works at Brough was responsible for building the nose; and the forward fuselage was the responsibility of Hatfield. Production arrangements for the wing were not then decided, and it was not until after the programme received the go-ahead again in July 1978, after being shelved, that a risk-sharing agreement was signed with Textron Aerostructures Inc (the former Avco Lycoming) for the manufacture of BAe146 wings at its Stratford, Connecticut, plant. By 1984 it was estimated that the current 146 order book had generated 900 jobs at Stratford and brought Textron business valued at £360 million. Another foreign firm brought into the 146 programme after it was revived was Saab-Scania of Sweden which, under a risk-sharing agreement signed on 8 December 1978, contracted to build the tailplane, elevators, rudder, ailerons, spoilers and all movable control surfaces, while design and manufacture of the engine pods was contracted to Short Bros at Belfast, the first pod being delivered to Hatfield in January 1981. Before the programme's suspension in October 1974, some talks had taken place with Aérospatiale over the possible manufacture of 146 wings by them at Nantes, but in the end nothing came of this.

In addition to the main design and sales mock-up, work continued apace at Hatfield in 1973-74 on detailed wooden mock-ups of the nose (for deciding flightdeck layouts and the location of electrical and avionic equipment), the front passenger door, the hydraulics bay and the wing leading ledge and centre section. The extensive metal engineering mock-up beside the Trident assembly line was the first mock-up of its kind for a Hawker Siddeley aircraft, although one was employed for the Airbus. The fail-safe airframe is designed for a crack-free life of 40,000 flights (representing 30,000hrs flying time), a life with minor repairs of 55,000 flights and a structural endurance, with major repairs, of 80,000 flights. Fatigue testing was due to start in October 1975 and to be completed by the end of 1976, and ditching characteristics were to be investigated and proven by model tests in a water tank.

Design Philosophy

The 146 was specifically designed to offer a jet replacement for the Viscount that could operate under the same conditions as tuboprops such as HS748s, F27 Friendships and Convairs then being used on short-haul feeder routes. The original timescale for certification and production corresponded with the period when a large number of these turboprops (possibly 800 or so) would be 10 years old, and several hundreds more would be at least 15 years old and in need of replacement. The 146 was designed to have direct operating costs per seat-mile, with five-abreast seating, some 15 per cent below those of the twin-turboprop types.

Since many of the airfields the 146 would operate from would be in difficult terrain, surrounded by mountains or other obstacles and without clearways or stopways, it was designed to have a large margin for obstacle clearance even with one engine failed. It was intended to have no limitations at airfield elevations up to 5,000ft and temperatures of ISA+20°, being able to use full take-off flap of 40° under these conditions at maximum gross weight; its field performance at high altitudes and temperatures is as good as, or better than, the twin-engined turboprops it was meant to replace. A low

BAe 146 Dimensions

	Series 100	Series 200	Series 300
*Span	86ft 5in	86ft 5in	86ft 5in
Length overall	85ft 11 1/2in	93ft 10in	101ft 8 1/4 in
Height	28ft 3in	28ft 2in	28ft 3in
Wing area (gross)	832sq ft	832sq ft	832sq ft
Aspect ratio	8.97	8.97	8.97
Fuselage diameter (external)	11ft 8in	11ft 8in	11ft 8in
**Max internal cabin width	11ft 1in	11ft 1in	11ft 2 1/2in
Max internal cabin height	6ft 7 1/2in	6ft 7 1/2in	6ft 7 1/2in
Max cabin length	50ft 7in	58ft 5in	66ft 3 3/4in
Floor width	10ft 6 1/2in	10ft 6 1/2in	10ft 6 1/2in
Total under-floor hold capacity	479cu ft	645cu ft	788cu ft

*Span of 86ft 5in includes static dischargers, which extend 2 1/2in from each wingtip
**Cabin dimensions exclude the flightdeck but include galley and toilets

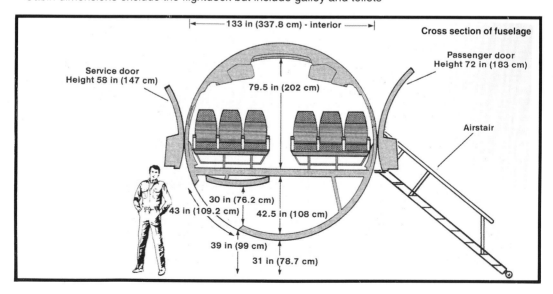

Left:
The fuselage had a circular cross-section with a maximum diameter of 11ft 8in. This allowed five-abreast seating as comfortable as that on many wide-bodied jets.

approach speed of just over 100kts simplifies approach procedures, while the folding petal-type airbrakes at the extreme rear of the fuselage allow precise height control on the approach and during touchdown. The ability to operate from short or unpaved semi-prepared strips with minimal ground facilities, and from runways of low pavement strengths, is an important feature of the 146, and low pressure tyres are offered as optional for such conditions.

Ease of maintenance was an important consideration aided by such keep-it-simple solutions as manual flying controls, except for the hydraulically-operated rudder and wing roll spoilers; the majority of systems components have been bought off-the-shelf. The ALF 502 engine pods with their upward-opening cowlings gave ease of access for maintenance and put all the main accessories at a convenient working height for ground crews. Avco Lycoming had recently set up a new division, Avco Lycoming Overseas Corporation, to handle the ALF 502's commercial side, and discussions had been held with several overhaul organisations and airlines on the subject of ALF 502 overhauls. After the 146 programme was halted in October 1974, work on the ALF 502M continued until the certification stage.

Technical Description

The 146 made use of design experience from the HS748, Trident and Airbus although, unlike the HS748, it made extensive use of high temperature-curing adhesive bonding — a technique well-established on all postwar Hatfield transports and especially the DH106 Comet. Wing aerodynamics were developed from Trident and Airbus technology, and the Hawker Siddeley high-lift aerofoil section allows a high-speed cruise of Mach 0.7 (315 knots) to be combined with a maximum lift coefficient of 3.38 without the need for high-lift devices such as leading edge flaps. The wing has 15° sweepback at the quarter chord line and 3° anhedral at the trailing edge; the thickness/chord ratio is 15.3 per cent at the wing root, decreasing to 12.2 per cent at the tip. The wing upper surface, which is normally subject to compression loads, is machined from L95 aluminium/zinc alloy, while the front and rear spars and bottom wing skins, which are subject to tensile and fatigue loads, are machined from L93 and 24S aluminium/copper alloy.

Large single-section tabbed Fowler flaps, of a total area of 210sq ft, span 78 per cent of each wing trailing edge and are operated by Dowty Rotol hydraulic actuators. The balanced ailerons are mechanically-actuated with a trim and servo tab in each one, and there is a hydraulically-operated roll spoiler on the upper surface of each outer wing, each spoiler operating when the aileron next to it moves down beyond a preset limit. Inboard of the roll spoilers are three other spoilers on each wing that act as lift dumpers, and can be set to extend automatically on touchdown. All six lift dumpers and both roll spoilers are identical for interchangeability. The wing leading edges are de-iced by hot air. The pylon-mounted engines help to relieve the bending and torsion felt by the wing during flight, as well as helping to ensure acceptable stall behaviour.

The absence of leading edge flaps also reduces the pitch changes that have to be balanced out by the tailplane, enabling a fixed-incidence one to be used, thus avoiding the complexity of the all-moving kind. The swept-back tailplane, which has an inverted NACA aerofoil section, is mounted on top of the fin mainly because this position has the greatest moment arm and so allows the smallest size of tailplane, but also because this ensures clearance from the jet exhaust and wing downwash. The manually-operated balanced elevators each have a trim and servo tab, and the rudder is hydraulically operated by two jacks. The tailplane leading edges, like those of the wing, have hot air de-icing, and this surface has chemically etched light alloy skins bonded to 'top hat' section stringers.

Thrust reversers on the engines were made unnecessary by the use of two hydraulically-operated petal-type air brakes below the rudder that form the tail cone when closed; their total area is 40sq ft, and each deflects through up to 60. These air brakes may be used at any time in flight to increase descent rate without the lift and pitch changes normally associated with wing-mounted brakes, but they are used mainly on the approach. BAe claims that these brakes are more than twice as effective as the wing-mounted ones on the McDonnell Douglas DC-9 or Boeing 737. The maximum descent rate that can be achieved with these brakes is no less than 7,000ft/min, and

BAe 146 Weights

	Series 100	Series 200	Series 200-QT	Series 300	Series 300-QT
Operating weight empty	49,559lb	51,294lb	48,925lb	53,951lb	50,965lb
Max payload	18,941lb	23,706lb	26,075lb	24,549lb	27,535lb
Max fuel weight (standard)	20,640lb	20,640lb	20,640lb	20,640lb	20,640lb
Max fuel weight (optional)	22,704lb	22,704lb	22,704lb	22,704lb	22,704lb
Max take-off weight	84,000lb	93,000lb	93,000lb	97,500lb	
Max zero-fuel weight	68,500lb	75,000lb		78,500lb	
Max landing weight	77,500lb	81,000lb		84,500lb	
Max wing loading (lb/sq ft)	101.0	111.8	117.2		
Max power loading (lb/lb st)	3.01	3.34	3.34		

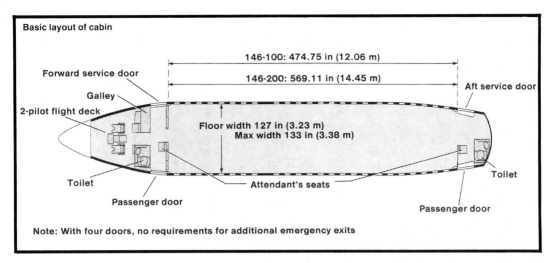

Basic layout of cabin

146-100: 474.75 in (12.06 m)

146-200: 569.11 in (14.45 m)

Forward service door

Galley

2-pilot flight deck

Aft service door

Floor width 127 in (3.23 m)
Max width 133 in (3.38 m)

Toilet

Toilet

Attendant's seats

Passenger door

Passenger door

Note: With four doors, no requirements for additional emergency exits

at speeds of less than 250kts and below 10,000ft there is still 4,000ft/min available. This compares with a typical airliner descent rate on the approach of around 2,000ft/min, and these powerful brakes, which can also be used in the landing roll, make steep approaches into awkwardly sited airfields surrounded by high ground that much easier.

The fuselage is a pressurised semi-monocoque structure with a diameter of 11ft 8in, a width chosen to provide five-abreast seating as comfortable as that on wide-body jets, from which in many cases passengers will transfer to their BAe146 regional flights. Maximum cabin width is 11ft 1in on the 146 Series 100 and 200, and 11ft 2½in on the Series 300, while the maximum cabin height is 6ft 7½in. As part of the philosophy of keeping down production and maintenance man-hours, and hence costs, the fuselage makes use of fewer parts, the nose and tail cone area being free of stringers, and there is only one main joint in the front fuselage, that between the nose and the centre section.

The fuselage is made entirely of aluminium/copper alloy, with naturally aged L109 alloy used in the pressure cabin and L90 alloy for those areas not subjected to pressurisation loads. Apart from the nose and tail cone, the rest of the fuselage has 'top hat' section stringers Redux-bonded to the skin above the keel area, while Z-section stringers are assembled with Thiokol bonding agent and riveted to skin in the keel area. The fuselage frames comprise an inner ring to take bending loads and an outer, notched ring that carries mainly shear loads, this arrangement allowing the elimination of about 5,000 stringer/frame cleats. With the introduction of the 146 Series 300, the strengthened centre-section originally developed for this version will become standard on all future Series 100s.

Composite materials have been used in only two areas of secondary structure — the wing/fuselage fillet and flap track fairings, both of which are of glass fibre-reinforced plastic. Two of the flap track fairings on each wing are in line with the engine pylons to reduce drag. Some idea of how successful BAe has been in keeping the 146 simple can be gauged from the number of structural drawings, which total about 9,000 compared to about 19,000 such drawings for the BAC One-Eleven and roughly 16,000 for the Trident. BAe has also claimed that the use of integrally-machined parts and Redux-bonding has saved around 120,000 fasteners on the 146.

Dowty Rotol designed the hydraulically retractable nosewheel undercarriage, which had to be tough enough to withstand operation from unpaved runways. There are twin Dunlop wheels on each unit and the main wheels, which are displaced outboard during extension, retract inwards into blister-type fairings on the lower fuselage sides. The steerable nosewheel retracts forward, and has a simple telescopic strut. Mainwheel tyre pressure for the 146 Series 100 is 122lb/sq in, while nosewheel tyre pressure for this variant is 113lb/sq in; as mentioned previously, low pressure tyres are optional. Dunlop supplied multi-disc carbon brakes for the mainwheels, these being operated by duplicated hydraulic systems. Carbon brakes, which are much lighter than the more traditional steel units, had only been used once before, on Concorde, and automatic braking may be preset to begin at touchdown. There are anti-skid units in both the primary and secondary brake systems.

There are two 3,000lb/sq in hydraulic systems to power the flaps, air brakes, undercarriage and brakes. Electrical power for the 28v DC system is provided by an AC generator on each outer engine. Backup power can be supplied by a generator on the Garrett AiResearch GTCP 36-100M auxiliary power unit, which may be used at heights of up to 20,000ft; the APU is normally used for air conditioning and electrical power generation on the ground, and BAe claims that this particular model is only about a third of the weight of competitive units, with only half their fuel burn — a very useful factor for a short-haul jet such as the 146, which would normally keep its APU running during turnround. An APU was at first an optional feature before work on the 146 was halted in October 1974.

A conventional flightdeck was chosen for the 146, because it was reasoned that the latest digital avionics and CRT (cathode-ray tube) cockpit displays would not have justified their cost for such an aircraft. The avionics options are conventional, and include a third VHF com (or communications) set to add to the dual VHF com, an area navigation system, Selcal (selective calling system), tape reproducer and single or dual HF Com sets. A Sperry Primus 90 weather radar is fitted in the nose, and there is also a ground proximity warning system.

The automatic flight control and flight guidance system comprises a Smiths SEP 10 autopilot, a Sperry flight director display and separate attitude reference for each pilot, and a Garrett thrust management system (or TMS). This TMS was built to BAe specifications, and is a limited-authority auto-throttle which helps to reduce the workload arising from four engines, while giving a saving in fuel of 1-2%. The TMS gives correct engine settings for take-off with the throttles fully forward, automatically ensuring equal thrust from each engine. For take-off, maximum thrust, cruise or flight idle, the TMS can trim the throttles to a preset engine rpm or turbine gas temperature. Landings and approaches to Category II minima are possible with the addition of extra equipment and wiring, but initially the 146 was certified for Category I landings.

The stall warning system comprises stick shaker (warning) and stick force (identification) elements, which provide soft and hard corrective stick forces at the approach of stall conditions. With the 146 Series 300 first revealed at the 1984 SBAC Show, a new fully digital autopilot and avionics system was featured with either EFIS (Electronic Flight Information System) cathode ray tube cockpit displays or more conventional instrument displays. The first Series 300 to be fitted with an EFIS flightdeck was G-OAJF, which first flew with this on 19 April 1989. The 146's Normalair-Garrett cabin environmental control system allows up to 40% of the cabin air to be filtered and recirculated, whereas the more usual method of air conditioning is to tap hot and cold bleed air from the engines, pass this through the cabin and then dump it overboard without recirculation.

The 6,700lb st ALF 502H turbofans originally selected for the 146 were replaced after the programme was reactivated in July 1978 by four of the 6,970lb st (maximum take-off) ALF 502R-5 variant; the letters ALF stood for Avco Lycoming Fan, although Avco Lycoming has now become Textron Lycoming. The ALF 502R with a reduced rating received FAA certification in January 1981 as the 6,700lb st (maximum take-off) ALF 502R-3 to power the 146, and was followed by the improved ALF 502R-3A, 'R-4 and 'R-5 variants certificated in 1982-83, and the ALF 502R-6 in 1984. By 1988 a total of 419 ALF 502 engines had flown 1,500,000hr in BAe146s. On-condition maintenance is usually employed, although a fixed TBO (Time Between Overhauls) of 4,000hr has been granted. The 7,500lb st (maximum take-off) ALF 502R-6 and 'R-7 variants are available for the 146 Series 300, as well as the ALF 502R-5.

The choice of four engines rather than two was originally dictated by the ALF 502's thrust and availability, but the use of four engines rather than two gives an important advantage in 'hot and high' conditions — a greater reserve of power with one engine out for obstacle clearance and a safe climb rate when taking off from short runways and using difficult airfields. Other advantages of having four engines instead of two include the ability to make three-engined ferry flights without passengers, enabling a 146 to be flown back to base for an engine change, which is much simpler and cheaper than doing it in the field, especially if the airfield is remote and difficult to access by surface transport. Also, if one of four engines fails, more than half the aircraft's electrical and hydraulic power is still retained. It may also be that passengers are likely to feel safer with four engines than with two, especially over rugged and mountainous terrain; this is sometimes jocularly referred to as 'the four funnel approach', a reference to the great and apparently unsinkable Atlantic liners of bygone days.

Total fuel capacity is 3,098US gal (2,580imp gal) in two integral wing tanks and a centre section tank, the latter with a vented and drained sealing diaphragm above the passenger cabin. The centre tank was at first optional when work on the 146 was halted in October 1974, but later became standard, optional tankage now taking the form of two auxiliary tanks in the wing root/fuselage fairings, with a combined capacity of 310US gal (258imp gal) giving a total capacity of 3,408US gal (2,838imp gal) The first 146 to have these optional wing root tanks was the Series 100, TZ-ADT, for the Government of Mali,

Typical seating layouts

146-100

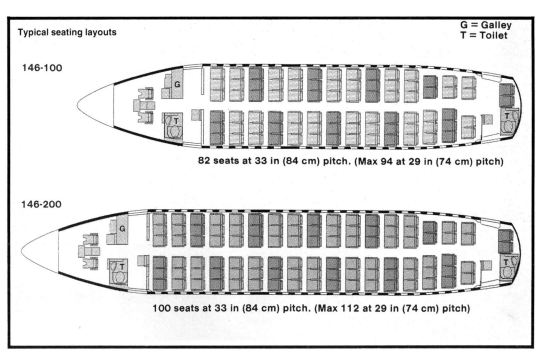

82 seats at 33 in (84 cm) pitch. (Max 94 at 29 in (74 cm) pitch)

146-200

100 seats at 33 in (84 cm) pitch. (Max 112 at 29 in (74 cm) pitch)

De-luxe commuter layout

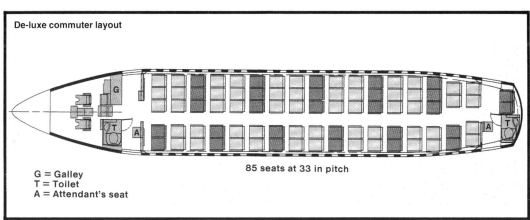

85 seats at 33 in pitch

G = Galley
T = Toilet
A = Attendant's seat

Mixed class layout

G = Galleys
T = Toilets
A = Attendants

146-200

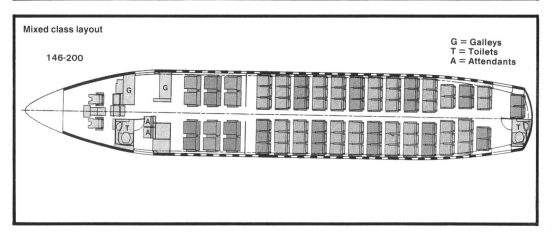

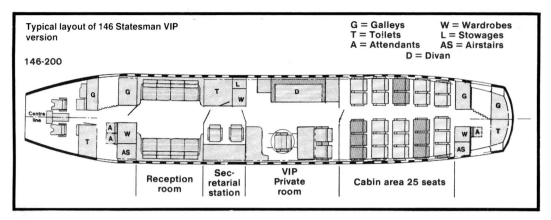

Typical layout of 146 Statesman VIP version

146-200

G = Galleys
T = Toilets
A = Attendants
D = Divan
W = Wardrobes
L = Stowages
AS = Airstairs

Centre line

| Reception room | Sec-retarial station | VIP Private room | Cabin area 25 seats |

which was delivered on 16 October 1983. Single-point pressure refuelling is standard, with a coupling situated in the starboard wing outboard of No 4 engine, and each wing also has an overwing filler. Fuel is fed to the engines by electrical pumps in the outer wing, with hydraulically driven pumps as backup. All the fuel-wetted areas of the wing are assembled with Thiokol sealant between the joints, which helps combat corrosion and avoids fuel leaks.

The flightdeck is laid out for two pilots, with provision for an optional observer's seat, and two or three cabin staff are carried. The 146 Series 100 can seat 82 passengers six-abreast at 33in pitch, or up to 93 passengers six-abreast at 29in pitch, or 71 passengers five-abreast at 33in pitch. The Series 200 can seat a maximum of 112 passengers six-abreast at 29in pitch in a high-density interior, or 100 passengers at 33in pitch. The Series 300 can seat 112 passengers at 31in pitch six-abreast in a slightly wider cabin, or 100 passengers four-abreast at 31in pitch (the standard layout), or up to 130 passengers in a high-density interior. A variety of alternative layouts are possible when the Series 300 is used in a mixed passenger/freight configuration.

All cabin interiors have two toilets and a forward galley as standard. However, four different galley installations are available to cater for the different needs of 146 airlines, ranging from short-stage commuter operations with minimum cabin service to two-hour sectors where full hot meals are served; for the latter requirement, four galleys can be installed, two forward and two aft, and Ansett WA is one airline that employs this galley fit in its 146s. Normally there are two toilets, one forward and one aft, but both may be located at the rear of the cabin, one in addition to, or as an alternative to, the forward toilet. Two different sizes of overhead luggage bin for passengers' carry-on luggage are available, the larger size for commuter operations where carry-on luggage loads are likely to be

greater, and an in-flight entertainment system is an optional feature.

The cabin length (excluding the flightdeck, but including the galley and toilets) is 50ft 7in for the Series 100, 58ft 5in for the Series 200 and 66ft 3¼in for the Series 300. There is one outward-opening passenger door forward and one aft on the port side of the cabin, both measuring 6ft 0in high x 2ft 9½in wide, and built-in airstairs are optional for both front and rear doors. Floor sill height of the forward door is 6ft 2in, and of the aft one 6ft 6in. Opposite these passenger doors are servicing doors, which also serve as emergency exits, one forward and one aft on the starboard side. For freight and baggage there are two holds under the cabin floor, forward and rear, with total capacities of 479cu ft in the Series 100, 645 cu ft in the Series 200 and 788cu ft in the Series 300. Each hold has one door in the starboard side, that of the forward hold being 3ft 7in high x 4ft 5in wide, and that of the rear hold being 3ft 5in high x 3ft 0in wide. Width of the cabin floor on all versions is 10ft 6½in. The windscreen has electrical anti-icing and demisting as standard, and a rain repellent system is optional.

The Project is Shelved
Meanwhile, as work on the HS146 proceeded during 1974, the political and economic storm clouds were gathering. The fuel price rises that had resulted from the Arab-Israeli Yom Kippur war of October 1973 were bringing about a worldwide recession, and for a time the OPEC countries (mainly Arab) led by Saudi Oil Minister Sheikh Yamani, seemed to hold the rest of the world by the throat, economically. At home, inflation had been rising (it had reached 17% by August 1974), and the miners' strike of 1972 marked a new era of militant trade union power that for a time seemed to threaten democratic government itself. The Tories under Mr Edward

Heath, running on a 'Who Rules Britain?' ticket, fought two elections in February and October 1974, both of which resulted in a Labour victory, the first a narrow one and the second more substantial. The electioneering atmosphere that prevailed throughout 1974, and Labour's pledge to nationalise the aircraft industry, did not make for certainty and confidence in planning the future of major industrial projects like the HS146. The world's scheduled airlines, hit by fuel price rises, forecast record losses for 1974 and faced 1975 with gloomy foreboding.

It was against this background that Hawker Siddeley came to the conclusion in October 1974 that the HS146 programme was no longer commercially viable. The prospect of work stopping led to a joint trades union committee, co-ordinated by Mr James Greening, being formed to try to save the aircraft and to lobby for political support for the programme. In the course of a few weeks this committee saw Hawker Siddeley chairman Sir Arnold Hall, Prime Minister Harold Wilson, Mr Edward Heath, now Leader of the Opposition and Mr David Steel, then Liberal Chief Whip, to put their case. This was that the HS146 was vital to the aircraft industry's future as, with manufacture of only 16 Concordes authorised, and all our other civil aircraft near the end of their development lives, work on the A300 Airbus wing and development of the 30-seat Short SD3-30 commuter airliner would be no substitute for a major new civil project. A total of about 400 people, mostly design and sales staff, faced the prospect of redundancy if the HS146 was cancelled, with Hatfield staff likely to be the worst hit. As work on the HS146 slowed to a halt (it was terminated unilaterally by Hawker Siddeley on 21 October), there were work-ins and demonstrations at Hatfield and Brough which included an occupation of the Brough drawing office.

On 4 November 1974, Left-winger Mr Tony Benn, Labour's Secretary for Industry, told the Commons that he considered that Hawker Siddeley's decision to stop work on the HS146 was 'in breach of contract', this referring to the original Government launching aid agreement of August 1973 which had enabled it to go ahead. Mr Benn said that the Government was not satisfied that Hawker Siddeley's reasons for stopping work were valid. A committee of senior civil servants was asked by the Government to collect information and views on the HS146 and report to the Cabinet in about three weeks. In a further statement to the Commons on 9 December, Mr Benn in effect put the HS146 on ice. Hawker Siddeley had said that it could only continue if the Government would provide all the funding, which would have amounted to

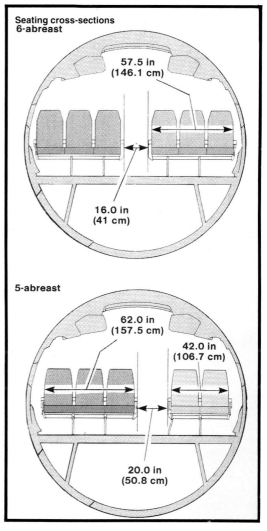

Seating cross-sections
6-abreast

57.5 in
(146.1 cm)

16.0 in
(41 cm)

5-abreast

62.0 in
(157.5 cm)

42.0 in
(106.7 cm)

20.0 in
(50.8 cm)

£120 million over three years at late-1974 prices. This the Government could not justify, but all jigs, tools and drawings, plus the design capacity would be maintained, if necessary with Government help, so that the 146 would be available for review by a future nationalised aircraft corporation.

The unions continued to press for full-scale continuation, and the Confederation of Shipbuilding and Engineering Unions (CSEU) made the point that 29 airlines had been visited by Hawker Siddeley teams up to that time, of which 13 had shown interest and sent their people to view the 146 mock-up, while 20 had asked for further information on route studies and performance. But for some time after Mr Benn's 9 December Commons statement, the HS146 situation remained fluid; when Hawker Siddeley ceased work on the 146 unilaterally on

BAe 146 Performance

	Series 100	Series 200	Series 200-QT	Series 300
Max operating speed	345mph	339mph		339mph
Economical cruising speed at 30,000ft	440mph	440mph	440mph	440mph
Cruising speed at 29,000ft for 345-mile sector	477mph) (high speed) 416mph (long range)	477mph (high speed) 416mph) (long range)		491mph (high speed) 434mph (long range)
Take-off run to 35ft, sea level and ISA	4,100ft	4,950ft		5,750ft
FAR landing distance from 50ft at sea level and ISA, max landing weight	3,500ft	3,620ft		4,030ft
Stalling speed with 33° flap at max landing weight	103mph EAS	106mph EAS		106mph EAS
Range with max standard fuel at 5,000ft, with reserves for 173 miles diversion and 45min holding	1,924 miles	1,698 miles		1,748 miles
Range with max payload (reserves as above)	1,077 miles	1,355 miles	1,381 miles	1,253 miles

21 October, it cancelled all the subcontracts to suppliers of a wide variety of things such as instruments, and claims by subcontractors against the company had to be met. An order for the first batch of 100 ALF 502 engines was cancelled, but this did not do lasting harm to the firm's relationship with Hawker Siddeley.

Gradually the winding-down of the HS146 project continued, design and research being kept going on a limited basis so as to be ready for future relaunching. On 2 December 1975 the Labour Government had its closest call of the new Parliamentary session when the Aircraft and Shipbuilding Industries Bill to nationalise these two industries achieved a second reading by a majority of only five votes — 280 'Ayes' and 275 'Noes' in Hansard's terminology, all the opposition parties joining with the Tories in voting against it. This Act, which established British Aerospace, finally passed through Parliament on 15 March 1977 and received the Royal assent two days later. On 29 April (which was vesting day), Hawker Siddeley was absorbed into British Aerospace, which continued to provide limited funding for the manufacture of assembly jigs, systems test rigs and for design and wind tunnel testing to go on. The 146 was the first new aircraft to be undertaken by the new British Aerospace, and henceforth became known as the BAe146.

Construction

The BAe146 was constructed by
British Aerospace at five factories.
The tail was made by SAAB in
Sweden. Avco built the wing at
Nashville, Tenessee.
These photographs show various
stages of construction and final
assembly at Hatfield.

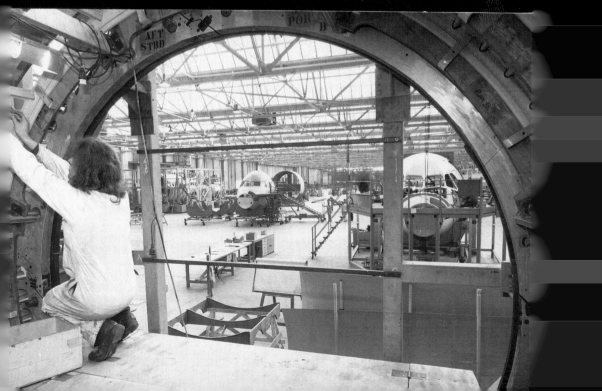

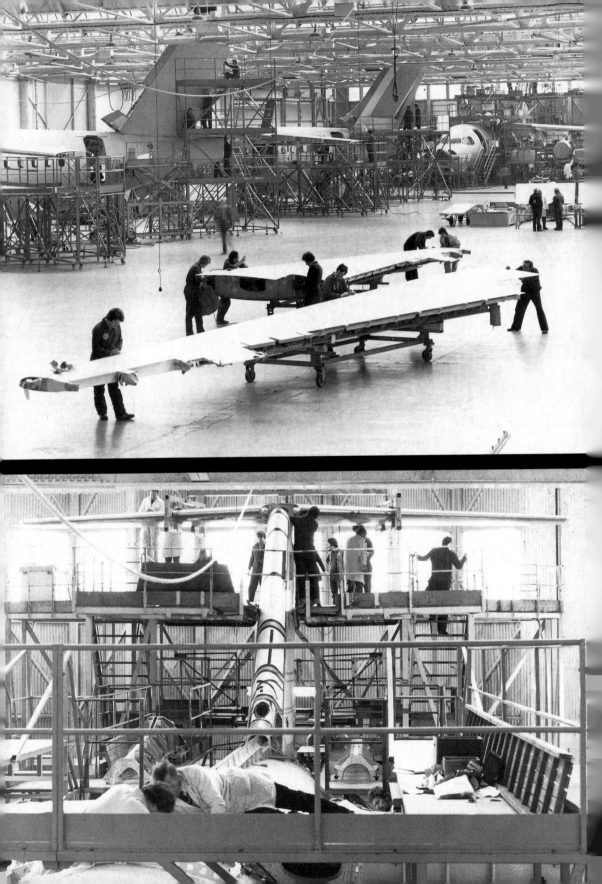

3 First Flight and First Orders

After the formation of British Aerospace (BAe), the 146 programme was subjected to a thorough review and the potential market for it was carefully reassessed. By the beginning of 1978 the economic picture was somewhat brighter, and the BAe board's decision to give the 146 programme the full go-ahead was announced in a statement to the Commons on 10 July 1978 by Labour Industry Minister Mr Gerald Kaufman, who gave the government's approval for the programme's restart in both the basic civil form and as a military freight version with a rear-loading ramp. The total non-recurring investment was estimated at £250 million, and it was expected that BAe would be able to find this sum from its own resources. Mr Kaufman also revealed that Avco, which supplied the engines, had also offered to manufacture the wings as a risk-sharing partner in the programme. The 146 should be worth 7,000 jobs to BAe and 4,000 to 5,000 jobs to suppliers, he said.

BAe started selling the 146 as a relaunched programme within hours of Mr Kaufman's Commons statement, wasting no time in telexing the news to all its potential airline customers; one such customer was actually visiting Avco Lycoming with a BAe team when the news broke. BAe had submitted its relaunch proposals to the government on 22 March, envisaging government approval in April and a first flight for the 146 Series 100 in time for the 1980 SBAC Show at Farnborough. This was later revised to November 1980 following the delayed approval, with the military freighter variant's first flight scheduled for August 1982. However, development of the latter was put back to enable priority to be given to the civil 146, and it was not until the 1987 Paris Salon Internationale that firm, details of military variants of the 146 were revealed. The original military version was to have been powered by the 7,500lb st Avco Lycoming F102 turbofan from which the ALF 502 was derived.

Now that the programme was relaunched, the problem arose of building up the design staff from the 270 then on the payroll to a total of 400. The aircraft industry had been hit by the Labour government's incomes policies, which had meant that some designers had had to leave for other better-paid jobs to improve their salaries, while others had gone to seek their fortunes outside aerospace because of the lack of stimulating new

work. BAe also had to renegotiate contracts with suppliers who had ceased work when the programme was halted in October 1974, and the original apportionment of production work between Hatfield, Manchester, Brough and other centres made in 1973 now had to be altered to take account of participation by Avco (now Textron Aerostructures Inc) and Saab-Scania of Sweden.

Avco's Aerostructures Division signed a risk-sharing agreement to build BAe146 wings at its Nashville, Tennessee, plant alongside C-130 Hercules and TriStar parts, the initial Avco contract calling for the supply of 20 wing sets, with two structural wing test specimens to be delivered to Hatfield in kit form in the latter half of 1979. The use of Avco-built wings as well as ALF 502 engines accounted for as much as 40% of the 146's content, even excluding the cost of spares (including spares, the figure would be higher, because the engines would account for a very large proportion of spares over the aircraft's life). But the Avco deal helped enhance the 146's sales prospects in the States at a time when the Americans were becoming sensitive about airliner imports, and the smaller US airlines in particular were less willing to defy pressures to buy American. At the time the programme was halted in October 1974, Aérospatiale had been given a contract to build 12 HS146 wings at its Nantes factory, and to do a small amount of detailing of production drawings, but the French firm did not resume negotiations with BAe when the 146 was relaunched.

As related in the previous chapter, Saab-Scania of Sweden signed a risk-sharing agreement on 8 December 1978 to build the 146's tailplane, elevators, rudder, ailerons, spoilers and all movable control surfaces, this representing an investment of about £70 million for the Swedish firm and providing work for about 300 people. Short Bros at Belfast, which was also producing engine pods for the Lockheed TriStar and Rolls-Royce RB211-powered Boeing 747s, received an initial £4-million contract for 20 sets of four engine pods for the 146, the first pod being delivered to Hatfield in January 1981. The former Scottish Aviation at Prestwick, now part of BAe, contracted to build the engine pylons, while the former Folland Aircraft Ltd factory at Hamble made the flap track fairings. The 146's centre fuselage is manufactured at Filton, the rear fuselage at Manchester, the fin and flaps at Brough, and the forward fuselage and flightdeck at Hatfield, which was, as before, the main design centre and also responsible for all final assembly and flight-testing. The latter responsibility began to be shared when the new 146 production line at Woodford, near Manchester, was set up in 1987-88.

Market Predictions

A first flight date for August 1980 was originally scheduled on the assumption of government approval for the relaunch being given in April that year, and six more Series 100 production aircraft were to fly in 1981, the eighth aircraft being the first Series 200. Break-even point on the 146 programme was expected to be reached at 250 aircraft sold, assuming that the US regional/commuter airline market could be penetrated, which in due course it was. Selling price was initially fixed at $7.5 to $8 million against a 1979 datum, and BAe claimed that aircraft-mile costs for the Series 100 would be 20% below what it described as a 'typical twinjet' (in fact this was an average of McDonnell Douglas DC-9 and Boeing 737 costs) on a stage length of 150 nautical miles (nm), assuming fuel costs of 44 cents/US gal. Seat-mile costs for the Series 100 would be from 10 to 30% below those of a turboprop twin in the F27 Friendship/Convair 580 class. BAe foresaw a market for 225 Series 100s and 135 Series 200s by 1990, based on the assumption that there would be no large-scale selling off of DC-9s and 737s in the 1980s. It was felt that about 80% of Series 200s sold would go to airlines that had already bought the 146 Series 100, and that 60% of all 146 operators would use six-abreast seating, even though this might be rather a tight squeeze for some passengers.

Such were some of the basic commercial calculations behind the 146 on its relaunch. As before, its economics were optimised around a very short stage length of 150nm, rather than the 350nm or more of twinjets like the 737 and DC-9; this meant that the 146 could employ low cruising speeds and a lightly swept wing without affecting block times. Apart from the wing centre section fuel tank now being standard, and new optional tanks in the wing root fairings, the 146 was basically unchanged from the form it took when work halted in October 1974 although, during the interval before relaunch, opportunity had been taken to refine the systems and structure, and to select better materials. A major study was also made to see if powered flying controls would be smaller, lighter or cheaper, but in the end manual controls were retained. It was intended to use three Series 100s and a single Series 200 for certification flying, the latter variant being certificated by mid-1982. A maximum production rate of three 146s a month was envisaged.

The sale of no less than 100 of the original military version of the 146 was assumed in the financial planning behind the relaunch, even though the RAF at that time had no requirement for such a transport. With a rear loading ramp that folded up into the rear fuselage, a strengthened freight floor and a loading strut under the rear fuselage just ahead of the ramp, the military 146 could have accomodated a CVR(T) Scorpion tank weighing 17,500lb and a half-ton truck; a one-ton truck, a 105mm field gun and a half-ton truck, or up to 70 fully-equipped paratroops. Optional long range fuel tanks of a total capacity of 486Imp gal could be fitted in the underfloor cargo holds. It was originally intended that rear-loading military variants of the 146 were to be developed and marketed at Manchester, but the potential market for these was to some extent pre-empted by the Spanish CASA C212 Aviocar and the CASA/IPTN CN-235, a

Below:
It was Air Wisconsin's initial order for four Series 200s plus four on option, announced the same day as the rollout ceremony on 20 May 1981, that really got the 146 programme off the ground commercially. N606AW Kitty seen here is named after the wife of Air Wisconsin's president.

co-operative venture between Spain and Indonesia; although much smaller designs than the 146, they were also cheaper and sold in some numbers to Third World air forces.

The 146 had been relaunched without any firm orders to back it, although an intensive sales effort was under way by BAe, and the only airline publicly to express an interest in the 146 before it restarted had been East-West Airlines Ltd of Tamworth, New South Wales, a small Australian operator that flew services mostly in New South Wales with a fleet that in 1979 numbered 11 F27 Friendships. In the end East-West did not place a 146 order until August 1989 when, now as part of the Ansett group, it signed for eight Series 300s. It was not until May 1981, nearly three years after the relaunch, that Air Wisconsin announced its first order for four Series 200s plus four on option; two earlier announced orders by other operators had lapsed, and so Air Wisconsin became the launch customer.

At the end of 1978, Dutch feelings about the 146 revived when both the Dutch Government and Fokker-VFW lodged official protests with the EEC Commission in Brussels against the decision to relaunch the 146, claiming that it was a threat to their Fokker F28 Fellowship and could have a negative influence on the good spirit of co-operation which had up to then existed between Fokker-VFW and the British aircraft industry. The Dutch also claimed that the BAe146's relaunch was 'in direct conflict with resolutions previously passed by the EEC', which referred to the non-duplication of civil aircraft projects, and they asked the Commission to examine the matter. This protectionist attitude on the part of the Dutch was uncharacteristic, as they had launched the Rolls-Royce Dart-powered F27 Friendship two decades before, at a time when the Vickers Viscount turboprop was in the ascendant, without any similar protest; the Friendship had sold well (nearly 700 at the time of the 146 protest), even though it too had been launched without the backing of any firm order.

First Orders

The first BAe146 order to be revealed was for three with an option on three more from Lineas Aereas Privadas Argentinas SA — LAPA, announced on 4 June 1980. LAPA operated third-level or commuter services in the province of Buenos Aires between La Plata and Pehuajo using three Swearingen Metro IIs, and so its 146 order represented a major expansion plan. Two of its 146s were to be Series 100s seating 86 passengers and the third (plus the three on option) were to be Series 200s seating 104 passengers. Pending delivery of these, two BAC

One-Elevens were to have been leased to LAPA later in 1980 but unfortunately LAPA was unable to get approval for the routes on which it planned to operate its 146s, and so the order lapsed, although options on the three Series 200s were retained for some time. Another factor that would have put paid to LAPA's 146 order was the outbreak of the Falklands war a few months before the scheduled delivery dates of September and October 1982 for the first three 146s; patriotic pressures would have caused the cancellation of LAPA's 146 order even if it had obtained the necessary route approvals. In 1983 LAPA had to return its two Short SD3-30s to the manufacturers because of the difficulty of getting spares following the UK's embargo on trade with Argentina. An order for two 146s from an undisclosed US airline was revealed in September 1980, for delivery in November 1982 and March 1983, but this order too later lapsed.

To one man more than any other must go the credit for getting the 146 off the ground commercially; this was Mr Preston Wilbourne, president of Air Wisconsin Inc, of Appleton, Wisconsin, near Chicago, whose order for four 146 Series 200s plus four on option was announced on 20 May 1981, for delivery beginning in March 1983. It was the intention of Mr Wilbourne, and other local businessmen, to bring jet services to Appleton and in so doing generally put it on the map and boost local industry. He chose the Series 200 seating 100 passengers for his commuter airline, and by becoming the 146 launch customer, he set a sales pattern that emphasised the stretched Series 200 rather than the smaller Series 100 which it had been assumed would dominate the sales picture for the first four years.

By the spring of 1984, nearly a year after its first 146 was delivered, Air Wisconsin was serving 16 cities in Wisconsin, Indiana, Michigan, Minnesota and Ohio. Sectors averaged only 35min flying time and schedules at that time called for each 146 to complete up to 14 sectors a day, including five flights into Chicago's O'Hare

airport where slot timing is critical. About a year after the first 146 delivery to Air Wisconsin, BAe Hatfield's divisional sales director J. A. 'Johnnie' Johnstone was to say: 'The far-sighted initiative of Wilbourne, coupled with US deregulation and the world economy, have totally changed 146 marketing philosophy', adding nevertheless that 'the -100's day will come'. Most orders for both Series 100s and 200s were in small numbers, usually an initial order for two or three with several subsequent repeat orders (a pattern characteristic of feederline types such as the 146), and the Pacific Southwest Airlines order for 20, plus 25 on option, is the largest single order to be placed to date.

Registrations G-BIAD to G-BIAG, and G-BIAJ, had been reserved on 28 July 1980 for the first five 146 Series 100s which served as production prototypes, but these were not taken up and the five were re-registered C-SSSH (the 1st), G-SSHH (the 2nd), G-SSCH (the 3rd), G-SCHH (the 4th), the registration G-SCHH also being applied to the 5th aircraft, which would have originally become G-BIAJ. These re-registrations were intended to emphasise the 146's quietness, rather on the lines of the 'Sch. . . . sch. . . you know who' slogan advertising Schweppes drinks that was current some years ago. Roll-out of the first 146, G-SSSH, which served as the prototype, took place at Hatfield on 20 May 1981, simultaneously with the BAe announcement of Air Wisconsin's initial order for four Series 200s with four on option. This roll-out was the first of a major new British airliner since that of the BAC One-Eleven almost 18 years before, and so was indeed a historic occasion.

The order book already stood at 13 aircraft plus 12 more on option; Westair Holdings of California had ordered six Series 200s with options on a further eight for use by its subsidiary, Pacific Express Airlines of Chico, California, for delivery beginning early in 1984. Two more undisclosed airlines, one in North America and the other in Europe, had also ordered three between them plus two on option. Airlines did not always wish to disclose their names as confirmation of a new order might depend on completion of financing arrangements or the gaining of route approvals which might be jeopardised by premature disclosure of new fleet plans. Pacific Express acquired seven ex-British United Airways One-Eleven 201s from British Caledonian in 1981 for use on its commuter routes mostly within the state of California, the first One-Eleven being delivered from Gatwick on 10 December 1981. The One-Elevens were regarded as a natural 'lead-in' to operations with the 146, but the latter order was at first postponed for one year, initially at the end of 1983, and then cancelled when Pacific Express ceased operations in February 1984, filing for Chapter 11 bankruptcy due to the cut-throat competition in the California commuter markets. Four of its One-Elevens were disposed of to Air Wisconsin.

First Flight

At last the great day arrived, and on 3 September 1981 BAe146 Series 100 G-SSSH made its maiden flight from Hatfield in the hands of BAe test pilot Mike Goodfellow, who said afterwards that the aircraft was 'remarkably stable, very responsive and delightfully quiet'. Mike Goodfellow with deputy pilot Peter Sedgwick, flight development engineer Roger de Mercado and instrumentation engineer Roger Hammond, had waited patiently for the early morning fog to

clear, and G-SSSH lifted off the runway at 11.54hr BST; the 146 was accompanied by a BAe125 'chase plane'. The crew had rehearsed their task in fast taxi runs the evening before, in one of which G-SSSH was actually airborne for a short while. After making two almost silent passes at 300ft for the benefit of the large crowd gathered on the airfield, G-SSSH came in for a perfect landing 1hr and 35min later. The maiden flight had started at a maximum take-off weight of 64,000lb, ballast being used to obtain an accurate weight and centre of gravity position, and G-SSSH took only 17sec from brake release to rotation.

It was flown in public for the first time on 12 September, demonstrating its STOL performance, manoeuvrability and quietness, and by the 13th it had completed five test sorties totalling 6hr 50min airborne time. Stability and control had been tested over the low-to-moderate speed range at various flap settings, each sortie being flown with a different (but nevertheless fixed) flap setting, the aircraft being reported as viceless and easy to fly. It was used primarily for handling tests with a crew of two pilots, a test manager and a flight observer. After 50hr flying time, more test instrumentation was installed and after 83 block hours were reached the final installation of flutter-testing equipment was fitted, as well as the tail parachute that was carried as a precautionary measure during the early stages of stall testing. The air brakes were removed to make way for the tail parachute, which was housed in the extreme rear of the tail cone. The second 146 Series 100, G-SSHH, also featured local reinforcement around the rear fuselage for mounting a tail parachute for use during low-speed handling tests. Certification was planned for the third quarter of 1982, by which time 1,000hr of flight-testing should have been clocked up by the first four 146s. An unusual and very valuable feature was the use of an on-board computer in the first 146 to provide an instantaneous readout of some of the flight-test data on a small television screen in the cockpit;

this enabled test engineers to tell straight away whether a particular test had been satisfactory. For fatigue testing on the ground, four major structural specimens were tested to more than 110,000 cycles; these were a virtually complete airframe minus the nose, a nose section, a centre section and wingbox, and a rear fuselage with fin and tailplane.

At first plans called for 18 aircraft to be completed by the end of 1982, plus the first three being used in the test programme, and a production rate of three a month was to have been reached by the end of 1983. It was intended that 146 assemblies would spend only 15 weeks on the production line before leaving it as a complete aircraft, one of the factors making this possible being the supply of major 146 assemblies like the fuselage centre-section complete with hydraulic pipes, control runs and electric cables, so that assembly then becomes a fairly simple affair of bolting the sections together and making the necessary connections. At the time of the first flight the basic selling price for an 82-seat 146 Series 100 was set at $10.5 million at 1981 prices, and $11 million for a Series 200 seating 100 passengers; a 115-seat Boeing 737-200 would have cost about $2 million to $3 million more, and it had a much higher fuel burn, as well as being a generally more complex aeroplane.

The second 146 Series 100, G-SSHH, first flew on 25 January 1982 and was used to prove the systems, the auxiliary power unit, the Garrett thrust management system, and the anti-icing and cabin temperature control systems. It later made two important demonstration and sales tours to the USA and the Far East, in 1984, and also to East Africa in 1986.

The anti-icing tests, after an initial period of proving the on-board ice protection, involved

Top:
G-SSHH flies behind and below Canberra B2 WV787 which created artificial icing conditions by spraying water from a spray rig under its tail, through which G-SSHH then flew.

Above:
For 146 icing trials Canberra B2 WV787, already fitted with the nose and cockpit of a Canberra B(I)8, was modified at Boscombe Down to have a water tank in the fuselage from which water was pumped via an under-fuselage pipe to a spray rig mounted just behind the tail cone.

Left:
A close-up of the tail of Canberra WV787 showing the spray rig from which water could be sprayed at pre-determined rates to enable the rate of ice build-up on the 146 to be carefully controlled.

making a number of flights behind Canberra B2, WV787, which — already fitted with the nose and cockpit of a Canberra B(I)8 — had been further modified at Boscombe Down with the addition of a water tank in the fuselage from which water was sprayed, via an under-fuselage pipe, from a bank of nozzles mounted just behind the tail cone, at pre-determined rates. This enabled the rate of ice build-up on the 146 flying behind and slightly below the Canberra, usually at about 200ft distance, to be carefully controlled, as it flew into the artificial icing conditions created by the Canberra. Accuracy in formation flying was essential so that water from the Canberra could be sprayed on to specific areas, and build-ups of ice could be observed on the outer wing leading edges, the engine intakes, the tailplane, windscreen and the extended undercarriage. A special probe was fitted that could be extended into the airflow ahead of the wing so that by photographing water droplets striking an oiled slide the water density could be confirmed. Ice accretion was photographed from cameras in the 146's cabin and also from a BAe125 'chase plane'.

These tests proved that the de-icing system could remove any ice build-up quickly, but it now had to be proved in natural icing conditions without the Canberra, and in search of these the 146 made the type's first overseas flight early in April 1982, to Reykjavik in Iceland, from where it made two flights, the track of the second taking G-SSHH north of the Arctic Circle and within 30 miles of the Greenland coast. Not long after the second 146, although its cabin was occupied by large water tanks, carried a small number of passengers to Berne in Switzerland to make its airshow debut; its performance on the 1,310m runway about 1,700ft above sea level made a most favourable impression on some 60,000 of the local citizens. On 25 August 1982 G-SSHH left Hatfield to undergo tropical trials at Madrid's military airfield of Torrejon which, at 2,000ft above sea level, was hot and high enough for this purpose.

The third 146 Series 100, G-SSCH, made its maiden flight on 2 April 1982 from Hatfield, and was used for performance evaluation; it was later leased to British Caribbean Airways in March 1986 and then to Pacific Southwest. The fourth

Above:
The third 146 Series 100, G-SSCH, seen here first flew on 2 April 1982 in an attractive dark brown, maroon, dull gold and white colour scheme.

Right:
The fourth 146 Series 100, originally G-SCHH, was re-registered G-OBAF for its intended customer British Air Ferries (BAF), in whose navy blue and white livery, with gold stripes, it is seen at the 1982 Farnborough show. It was used for route-proving trials from Southend at the end of 1982 flown by BAF pilots, but in the end BAF did not translate its letter of intent for 10 146s into a firm order.

146, G-SCHH, first took to the air on 29 August 1982 and was used for route proving trials; it was intended as the first to go to a customer. It was re-registered G-OBAF on 28 May 1982 and was based at Southend for a month from 7 December that year on route-proving flights; it was painted in British Air Ferries livery, this operator having announced a letter of intent to buy 10 146s at the 1981 Paris Salon Internationale. BAF applied to operate routes from London Heathrow to Innsbruck in Austria, Cannes, the ski resorts of St Moritz/Samaden and also to Tarbes in France, but in 1983 the air transport side of BAF underwent a change of ownership and in the end

Below:
The first 146 Series 200, G-WAUS (formerly G-WISC), in the livery of Ansett subsidiary Airlines of Western Australia (or Air WA) taxies out to the Farnborough runway for its demonstration at the 1984 SBAC Show. *M. J. Hardy*

Bottom:
The fourth and fifth 146 Series 100s, G-OBAF and G-SCHH respectively, served with No 10 Squadron, RAF, at Brize Norton as ZD695 (on the left) and ZD696, as BAe146 C Mk1s, partly to evaluate the 146 for possible use by the Queen's Flight.

no146 order was placed. The fifth 146, which was the second to bear the registration G-SCHH, first flew on 19 October 1982 and left Hatfield 14 days later on the first 146 overseas sales and demonstration tour, to the Far East and Australasia, which lasted until 13 December.

The 8th 146 was the first Series 200, registered G-WISC in honour of its first customer, Air Wisconsin, whose livery it wore; this first flew on 1 August 1982. Two years later it was re-registered G-WAUS (after a short spell with the Class B registration G-5-146) and repainted in the livery of Ansett subsidiary Airlines of Western Australia for the 1984 SBAC Show. For the 1986 SBAC show it became G-BMYE and later gave a demonstration of its quietness and STOL capabilities at the London City Airport on 24 July 1988. It did not go to a customer, being retained by BAe for test and demonstration purposes, but at the end of 1988 it was refurbished with a view to being sold.

Meanwhile, type certification of the 146 Series 100 was received from the UK Civil Aviation Authority (CAA) on 4 February 1983, followed by Transport category certification from

the American FAA on 20 May that year. By the end of August, the first nine 146s to fly had amassed a total of 5,000hr flight time, and the extensive test programme had resulted in lower than expected fuel burns, with consequent benefits to performance. Later production Series 100s have a thicker skin on the centre fuselage to permit increased take-off weight if required. The Series 200 also received its CAA transport category certification on 4 February, the same day as the Series 100, and altogether BAe spent around £350 million on the launch and certification of these two major variants. The prototype 146, G-SSSH, flew its last flight as a Series 100 on 7 August 1986, by which time it had flown 1,239.25hr and made 1,600 landings. It went for conversion into the stretched Series 300 aerodynamic prototype on 10 August, first flying in this new form as G-LUXE on 1 May 1987.

The second 146, G-SSHH, was re-registered G-OPSA on 20 January 1984 and, after its Far East sales tour, was leased to Pacific Southwest Airlines (PSA) as N5828B from 12 October 1984 until the following March, to provide PSA with an aircraft for crew training and with extra capacity, while its fleet of 20 146s built up to the full total; it was restored as G-SSHH on 25 March 1985. In June the following year it was leased to another US carrier, Aero West Airlines Inc (trading as Royal West Airlines) as N801RW. The fourth 146, after its spell of route-proving flights from Southend as G-OBAF, was cancelled on 3 May 1983 on sale to the RAF as ZD695, being delivered on 16 September. Together with the fifth 146 (the second G-SCHH), which was handed over to the RAF at Hatfield on 14 June 1983 as ZD696, it was used by No 10 Squadron at Brize Norton both as a staff and VIP transport seating 80 passengers, and also for evaluating the 146 for its possible use by the Queen's Flight to replace the ageing Andover CC Mk 2s used for so long as Royal transports. These first military 146s were known as BAe146 C Mk 1s, and they proved sufficiently successful with No 10 Squadron to result in an order for two BAe146

CC Mk 2s for the Queen's Flight, which were delivered in 1986. ZD696 was returned to BAe and leased to Dan-Air Services Ltd for three months from 16 July 1984 as G-SCHH; on completion of this lease it was purchased by Dan-Air to supplement its first two Series 100s in service, and was based at Newcastle. The other RAF 146, ZD695, was also leased to Dan-Air as G-BRJS (after a short spell as G-5-04) from 26 April to 15 November 1985; it served as a standby aircraft and was leased again by Dan-Air from 23 May to 7 June 1987.

Dan-Air Begins 146 Operations

Dan-Air Services Ltd had been the first British independent airline to announce a firm commitment to the 146 when, in September 1982, it ordered two Series 100s with an option on two more. It took delivery of the 6th 146, G-BKMN (previously G-ODAN) on 23 May 1983, this being the first 146 to be delivered to a customer, and this was followed by the 7th 146, G-BKHT, on 18 June. Dan-Air's first 146 service, from Gatwick to Berne in Switzerland, was actually flown on 1 March by the fourth 146, G-OBAF, borrowed from BAe, and G-BKMN flew its first Gatwick-Berne service on 27 May; it was based at Gatwick while G-BKHT flew services from Newcastle and Teesside.

As the first airline to put the 146 into scheduled service, Dan-Air found its entry into service very smooth, and was soon clocking up 8hr or more a day on a mix of scheduled and charter operations. Apart from some minor troubles with the engine starters, during which BAe made available an ex-Air Manchester One-Eleven as a back-up aircraft, Dan-Air found the 146's introduction singularly trouble-free, even though its first two 146s were based separately at Gatwick and Newcastle with all the potential headaches that that involved. By the summer of 1984, Dan-Air 146s were flying scheduled services to Dublin, Berne, Toulouse, and to Bergen and Stavanger in Norway, as well as operating charters. The 146 was the only jet

Top:
Dan-Air's G-BKMN seen here, the 6th Series 100, was the first 146 to be delivered to a customer, and flew its first commercial service, from Gatwick to Berne, on 27 May 1983.

Above:
The fourth 146 Series 100, G-BRJS, which started life as G-SCHH and later became ZD695 of No 10 Squadron, is seen in May 1987 near the end of a spell on lease to Dan-Air and just before going on lease to SATA of the Azores on 27 July that year. It later became G-OJET of Manx Airlines.
Leo Marriott

capable of using Berne's 1,310m runway, and when Dan-Air had first started flying there in 1972 it had had to use HS748 turboprops.

The 146's STOL capabilities made possible services to two new winter ski resort destinations, namely Innsbruck in the Austrian Tyrol and Chambery/Aix-les-Bains in the French Alps, which in December 1984 were added to the other places served by Dan-Air charters; both ski resorts were benefiting from British jet operations for the first time. By January 1985 Dan-Air had flown its one millionth 146 passenger, while in December that year Innsbruck began to be served by scheduled flights as well as charters. By 1987 Dan-Air was getting a daily utilisation of 8½ to 9hr from each of its 146s, and average sector length was only about 65min; seating was

for 86-88 passengers six-abreast, and three cabin crew were carried. A 146 Series 300, G-BPNT, was delivered on 2 June 1989 to supplement the Series 100s.

Avco Lycoming was quite as much on trial as BAe during the 146's commercial debut, for the name of Lycoming, although well known in general aviation and private flying circles, was far less familiar to airlines, and the ALF 502 was its first engine for a major airliner type. Avco Lycoming had to satisfy airlines used to the very high standards of Rolls-Royce and the other big engine names that they could respond quickly and effectively to any technical problem that arose, and this they were able to do. The first year's in-service, in-flight shutdown rate for the ALF 502 of 0.095 per thousand hours was much better than projected, according to BAe, and the performance achieved in the first year's 53,000 engine hours helped to confer the 146 with a despatch reliability rate 'as good with four as the 737 achieves with two', according to Avco. No engine delivered to Hatfield in the first year had failed to meet the specific fuel consumption target of 0.406lb/lb/hr for the ALF 502R-5; most engines of this variant achieved between 0.399 and 0.400lb/lb/hr, this fuel burn giving the 146 Series 200 a cruise consumption of 600 US gal/hr.

The first overseas sales and demonstration tour by 146, to the Far East, Australia and New Zealand, was undertaken by the fifth Series 100, which was the second to be registered G-SCHH, and this tour got under way before the type was certificated by the UK Civil Aviation Authority. This sales trip was aimed in particular at the Japanese domestic airlines, and a great deal of planning went into it; G-SCHH, with only 10hr of production test-flying behind it, was fitted with 74 passenger seats at 33in pitch and extra galley space to provide for full meal service on the long ferry stages. More than a ton of spares was carried to cater for any likely 'snags' during some 180hr of demanding flying, and a large amount of sales and promotional literature and catering stores were also on board. Overall tour manager was Capt Bob Hornall, marketing liaison manager at Hatfield, and Peter Sedgwick, Hatfield/Chester division deputy chief test pilot, was in charge of the flying aspects of the tour; the flight crew was completed by two 146 training captains, and various sales personnel and service representatives were also carried.

Thus equipped, G-SCHH left Hatfield at 13.20hrs GMT on 24 October 1982 and, flying via Bridisi in southern Italy, Larnaca (Cyprus), Bahrain (a diversion due to fog) and Dubai, arrived at Delhi the next day. G-SCHH left the following morning and, flying via Dacca and Bangkok, arrived in Hong Kong, where two Cathay Pacific stewardesses joined the cabin staff of two British Airways stewards, and final preparations were made for demonstrations in Japan. On 28 October the 146 arrived at Okinawa's Naha International Airport at the tail end of a rain squall, and the flight crew and sales executives disembarked to be presented with sprays of flowers by stewardesses of Southwest Airlines, the local airline of Okinawa. Both executives of the latter and members of the press and local dignitaries were given flights in the 146, which then left for Tokyo's Narita Airport via Nagoya. A stop for refuelling was made here as fuel uplift at the new Narita Airport was limited to scheduled flights; the local people had never been happy with the new airport and it had been the target of demonstrators and attempts had been made to stop trainloads of fuel reaching the airport bunkers. On the 30th, the 146 flew from Narita to the coastal town of Sendai with a load of TV and press men aboard; after refuelling at Sendai a second press flight was made from Narita to Tokyo's older international airport at Haneda.

On 1 November the 146 made two flights carrying senior executives and pilots of Toa Domestic Airlines, one of the major domestic operators, and on the second of these it landed at the resort of Nanki Shirahama, where the runway was only 3,940ft (1,200m) long; the 146 used less than half the runway on landing, repeating a similarly remarkable STOL performance on a second flight. Two YS-11 turboprops of the sort used by Toa Domestic, which landed at Nanki Shirahama after the 146, used the full runway length. That morning the 146 experienced its only technical 'snag' of the tour when a fault occurred in a flap computer; a new unit was installed and tested without the passengers having to disembark. The next day, further demonstration flights were made for

Below:
Named Nioro de Sahel, 146 Series 100, TZ-ADT, for the Government of Mali in West Africa was the first of the type to be exported, and was also used for commercial airline services by Air Mali, both to other West African countries and to Paris.

executives and pilots of All Nippon Airways, the major Japanese domestic airline, whose pilots were able to try the 146 for themselves in the Nanki Shirahama circuit. The 146's operations into this airfield were fully approved by the Japan Civil Aviation Bureau — JCAB, and it is worth noting that neither the DC-9 Series 40 or 80 nor the Boeing 737-200 were permitted to operate into or out of runways of Nanki Shirahama's length.

On 3 November HRH Prince Philip, who was in Japan in his capacity as President of the World Wildlife Fund, joined the 146 for a flight from Haneda to Sapporo's Chitose Airport, this city being the capital of Hokkaido in northern Japan, which is the most northerly of the nation's four main islands. Prince Philip is an experienced and knowledgeable pilot and, after spending some time on the 146's jump seat, he moved over and took the controls for most of the 1hr 40min flight to Sapporo, so becoming the first member of the Royal Family to fly on the 146. Among the other passengers were the chairman of BAe, Sir Austin Pearce, and the British ambassador to Japan, Sir Hugh Cortazzi. The next morning Prince Philip was again on the flightdeck for a short flight from Chitose Airport to Kushiro, where he was due to visit a wildlife park. Later that day the Royal party returned in the 146 to Tokyo's Narita Airport.

On 5 November the 146 flew to Osaka, Japan's second largest city and one of the most noise-conscious communities in the world, to make two local flights for the purposes of noise measurement, for which the Japanese set up no less than 23 noise measuring points instead of the usual 10. The 146 was carrying a load equivalent to 91 passengers and fuel for a 400-mile sector, and measurements were taken not only of the British jet, but of all the other types using Osaka airport, some of them much larger than the 146. BAe's claims that the 146 was the world's quietest jet airliner were fully vindicated by measurements taken at Kushiro Primary School, about 5,000m from the start of the take-off run; at this point the 146 recorded 76.6dBA (decibels absolute), the DC-9 86dBA, the L-1011 TriStar 88.3dBA, the A300 Airbus 90dBA, the Boeing 737-200 91dBA and the Boeing 727-200 96.5dBA, the figure achieved by the 146 being slightly less than those of the much smaller YS-11 turboprop (80.1dBA-82.2dBA). Since every 3dBA increase doubled the noise, it was not perhaps surprising that a number of measuring points reported that the 146 could not be distinguished from the noise of taxiing aircraft. After flying to Fukuoka for another demonstration flight for the local press and TV, the 146 went on to Okinawa to clear customs before leaving for Manila in the Philippines, where a demonstration flight was given. The 146 then flew on to Baguio, summer capital of the Philippines, where it landed in less than half the available runway length of 5,500ft, the runway being set high in the mountains, with a sheer drop of several hundred feet at either end.

From Manila the 146 flew on to Perth, Western Australia, via Brunei, Bali in Indonesia and Port Hedland, arriving at Perth on 10 November in the highest temperatures the city had experienced for 25 years. From Perth the 146 flew on to Canberra via the gold-mining town of Kalgoorlie in the Western Australian outback, and Adelaide; demonstration flights for government ministers and officials were given at Canberra, while the 146's low noise levels attracted much favourable comment, as they also did at Sydney. The 146 then visited Tamworth, New South Wales, home of East-West Airlines Ltd which had been the first customer to express publicly an interest in the 146 before its first flight, and which was finally able to order it seven years after Tamworth citizens first set eyes upon it. The 146 then called at Armidale and then Sydney and Melbourne; demonstrations were given at Melbourne to senior executives of Ansett and Trans Australia Airlines — TAA (now Australian Airlines), the two major Australian domestic carriers, and these were later to bear fruit in Ansett group orders for the 146.

The 1,500-mile flight from Melbourne to Christchurch, New Zealand, took 3hrs 14min, and was the longest of the tour. On 17 November G-SCHH flew into the 5,100ft runway serving the ski and tourist resort of Mount Cook in the South Island in crosswinds gusting up to 40mph, conditions which prevented the 748 turboprops of Mount Cook Airlines from landing there. The 146 then flew to Wellington, New Zealand's capital, for demonstrations to senior government ministers and airline representatives, then going on to Auckland where it completed the most intensive day's flying of the whole tour in spite of severe winds. While in New Zealand the registration ZK-SHH was allotted to the 146 to comply with local regulations concerning markings carried by an aircraft (in this case G-SCHH) which did not yet have a full C of A; but in the event the New Zealand registration was never actually carried by the 146.

On 20 November, G-SCHH left Auckland for Port Moresby, capital of Papua New Guinea, stopping at Nouma in New Caledonia, Port Vila in Vanuatu and the Solomon Islands. At Port Moresby the 146 was demonstrated to Air Niugini and the country's major third-level operator, Talair, while at Garoka airfield the 146 was surrounded by thousands of local tribesmen who touched and stroked the aircraft. The 146 arrived at Kuala Lumpur, capital of Malaysia, on the 25th, where it was demonstrated to Malaysian Airline System — MAS, and on 30 November it arrived at Delhi for a series of demonstration flights to Indian Airlines Corporation — IAC, and the other domestic airline, Vayudoot. Further demonstrations were made to Pakistan International Airlines in Karachi, Oman Aviation Services in Muscat and Kuwait Airways in Kuwait, and the 146 finally touched down at Hatfield at 15.00hrs on 13 December, on time to the day and minute after a tour lasting 51 days. During this the 146 had visited 20 countries, made 131 flights and carried 3,300 passengers in demonstration flights to 31 airlines with only one technical snag.

Wherever it went, and especially in Japan, the 146 had aroused great interest among both media and airline personnel on account of its extreme quietness and its ability to operate into airfields with short runways where no jet, let alone a four-engined one, had ever been before; reliability, too, had been outstanding. The 146 had come through the stringent noise measurement tests at Osaka with flying colours, and had proved itself to have a better STOL performance than the YS-11 turboprops used by several Japanese airlines; yet in the end no 146 order was placed by a Japanese carrier not least because that country, then as now, was very reluctant to admit significant imports of new foreign technology. But the 146's quietness had been publicly demonstrated and was later to prove a major selling point in the United States. As related in the previous chapter, G-SCHH went to the RAF in June 1983 as ZD696 and was later acquired by Dan-Air.

First 146 Exports

The first 146 Series 100 to be exported (and the ninth to be built) was TZ-ADT 'Nioro de Sahel' for the Government of Mali for use as a VIP transport by the President, government ministers and officials, and also for scheduled airline services by Air Mali, the national airline. Mali, formerly the French Sudan in what was French West Africa, is a landlocked country extending to just under 465,000sq miles. Leaving Hatfield on 15 October 1983, TZ-ADT flew via Seville in Spain and Las Palmas in the Canaries, arriving at Bamako, capital of Mali, on the 16th at 11.00hrs. After import formalities were completed, the 146 flew a party of VIPs headed by the Mali Presidency's Cabinet Director to Nioro, the community after which it had been named, and became the first jet to land on the narrow compacted gravel strip there, being greeted by a

large turnout of the local people. The next day it flew to the historic town of Timbuktu, a focus of the old caravan routes, and during its first two weeks in Mali the 146 was used extensively for Presidential visits to neighbouring African states, including Upper Volta, the Niger Republic, Guinea-Bissau, Senegal and Mauritania.

TZ-ADT was the first 146 to have the optional wing root fuel tanks and also the first to have a quick-change mixed-class cabin allowing flexibility of use in either the Presidential/VIP transport role, or for airline use with high-density passenger seating for up to 87 people. For its delivery flight, TZ-ADT's forward cabin was fitted with eight de luxe first-class seats, and a polished wood conference table was installed especially for the President's use. After its initial spell of Presidential use, the 146 was fitted with high-density seating for use by Air Mali on services to Lagos, Abidjan in the Ivory Coast and the Congo capital of Brazzaville, also operating the weekly Air Mali service to Paris. The engines, too, proved able to contend with the alternating dust storms and torrential rain in Mali, so contributing to TZ-ADT's 100% on-time despatch reliability record. Sadly, Air Mali later ran into financial difficulties and by 1988 had ceased operating its own services; TZ-ADT was returned to BAe and was put into storage at Chester.

Next customer to put the 146 Series 100 into service was the Brazilian regional airline Transportes Aereos da Bacia Amazonica — TABA, based at Belem near the mouth of the Amazon and serving over 30 destinations in northwest Brazil, including Manaus, the regional capital, La Cuiaba, some 700 miles south and Ji Parana, about 800 miles to the west. TABA had ordered two 146s with an option on three more, and the first of these, PT-LEP (formerly G-BKXZ), was handed over at Hatfield on 5 December 1983, flying its first TABA scheduled service, between Belem and Porto Velho, on 2 January 1984, followed by the second, PT-LEQ, shortly after. The two were soon serving nine destinations on TABA's network, replacing Fairchild FH-227B turboprops, and several more places were later added to the 146 schedules flown by TABA to provide better connections with larger Brazilian airlines. The 146s allowed TABA to offer the benefits of jet speed while keeping fares at competitive levels, thanks not least to their modest fuel consumption, which was a major factor in TABA's choice of the 146.

Before entering regular service TABA's first 146, PT-LEP, had operated a series of demonstration flights from Rio de Janeiro in conjunction with British Aerospace, and it became the first four-jet airliner to use the 4,200ft-runway of Rio's Santos Dumont Airport,

Left:
Air Pac 146, N146AP, seen on a pre-delivery test flight over England.

which had previously limited airlines to using propeller-driven types. The 146 also flew the route of the well known Ponte Aerea (Air Bridge) shuttle service from Rio's Santos Dumont to Sao Paulo's Airport at Congonhas, demonstrating its potentialities for the 'Ponte Aerea' which was operated by the three major Brazilian airlines Cruzeiro do Sul, Varig and VASP in pool using Lockheed Electra turboprops; the original Rio-Sao Paulo route was later supplemented by another 'Ponte Aerea' service between Rio, Belo Horizonte and Brasilia, the capital.

TABA's hopes for expanding its routes to the USA and Columbia had centred around the 146, but sadly its plans for the British jet were to founder over the question of spares provisioning. Although the airline's founder and president, Col Gibson Jacques, had complained that TABA's after-sales relationship with BAe and Avco Lycoming had not been good, leading to problems with the replacement of spare parts, the real problem had been TABA's refusal to pay the high tariffs the Brazilian government was demanding in duty tax (no less than 100%) to enable spare parts to be delivered. Unless this duty was paid, spares would not be allowed into the country. TABA's refusal to pay meant that two months after 146 operations had started, only one of them was still flying and late in 1985 both were returned to BAe after having been grounded for lack of spares for a whole year. BAe had offered an extremely attractive deal to win the TABA order, in which the airline was to pay US $40 million for its two 146s over a 10-year period; no down-payment was made, just US $2 million for the spares.

TABA was not a wealthy airline and the people of the Amazon valley which it served are very poor; in ordering the 146, TABA had also had in mind markets in Venezuela, Central America and the southern USA, especially Miami and Dallas. It had also considered the potential of cargo flights to the USA which would have been especially useful for transporting oil drilling rig equipment, and for which the 146 Series 200QT freighter would have been a natural choice. The two 146s had been well-liked by TABA passengers but no solution could be reached over the spares problem; PT-LEP was returned to BAe at Hatfield on 6 November 1985, later receiving the Class B registration G-5-512, and PT-LEQ had arrived at Hatfield six days before, later becoming G-5-513. Both 146s later went to the US regional airline Aero West (Royal West Airlines), PT-LEP becoming N802RW and PT-LEQ becoming N803RW.

The next 146 Series 100 customer was Air Pac Inc (Air Pacific Airlines) of Dutch Harbour in the Aleutian Island chain that stretches from Alaska towards Siberia; the Series 100, N146AP, left Hatfield on delivery via Prestwick and Reykjavik on 3 March 1984, being subleased to Air Pac by Business Jet Aviation. Air Pac had been formed in 1978 at Dutch Harbour as an air taxi operator, and had become the dominant carrier between Anchorage and Dutch Harbour Unalaska since starting scheduled services between these points on 1 February 1982 providing daily connections with intra-Alaskan flights and services to the main part of the USA (the 'Lower 48' as Alaskans call it) operated by Alaska Airlines and other major carriers. Air Pac's 146 provided the first scheduled passenger jet service to the Aleutians, cutting the Dutch Harbour-Anchorage flight from 3hr to 1hr 55min and was certificated to use unpaved airfields and for extended overwater operations; it supplemented Air Pac's existing fleet of one

Fairchild FH-227, one Fairchild F27 Friendship, three Grumman Goose amphibians, one Swearingen Metro II and one Cesna Conquest. In addition to Dutch Harbour, Kodiak, Dillingham and King Salmon were also served on a scheduled basis by Air Pac.

The airline carried a considerable amount of freight, and the 146's cabin was fitted to seat either 76 passengers at 33/32in pitch, or a mixed payload of 40 passengers in the rear part of the cabin and four freight containers, which could each carry 1,500lb of cargo, in the forward part of the cabin. Both forward and aft galleys were featured for hot food service and the rear passenger entrance door had airstairs. Among the cargoes flown out of Dutch Harbour's unsealed 3,950ft crosswind gravel strip, which ends in the sea and runs through what used to be the side of a hill, were loads of king crabs destined for dining tables on the Alaskan mainland. Flying weather in the Aleutians was among the worst in the world, with fog, rain, sleet, snow and low visibility to contend with, yet in spite of this Air Pac was getting a daily utilisation of just over 5hr from its 146 by the end of July 1984, which had flown 763hrs with the airline; this was the third highest utilisation of any 146 operator at that time. But sadly, Air Pac ran into financial difficulties and in May 1986 suspended all its services; the 146, after going to AAR Inc at Oklahoma City for an overhaul and some modifications, was returned to BAe. It was leased to Pacific Southwest Airlines on 15 December 1986 for six months, and in 1988 was leased for a time to Westair Commuter Airlines.

Three years after Air Pac ceased operations and filed for Chapter 11 bankruptcy protection, three of its former executives filed a $100-million lawsuit against BAe and Textron Lycoming in October 1989, claiming that the 146's operating costs drove it into bankruptcy, and that early development problems with the 146 and its ALF 502 engines resulted in excessively high maintenance costs and a loss of millions of dollars of revenue while the 146 was grounded. The three ex-Air Pac executives also claim that BAe and Avco knowingly misled them about the 146's reliability and potential profitability, and concealed the fact that problems relating to the engines' performance had occurred during the 146's development. Both BAe and Textron Lycoming are contesting the case, and no other 146 operator has found similar legal action necessary; the 146's daily utilisation of 5hr in its first few months of Air Pac service does not seem to suggest unreliability and excessive time on the ground.

Air Wisconsin Operations
Air Wisconsin's first 146 Series 200, N601AW, left Hatfield on 16 June 1983 on delivery through Prestwick and Keflavik. It was followed by N602AW on 29 September, N603AW on 17 December and N604AW on 23 February 1984, so completing the initial order for four; the first 146 scheduled flight was flown by N601AW on 27 June. Air Wisconsin was no stranger to British aircraft; it had started operations in 1965 with two nine-passenger DH104 Doves, three pilots and 17 ground personnel, flying services into Chicago from the Wisconsin towns of Appleton and Neenah/Menasha. After about three years Minneapolis/St Paul was added to the network, followed not long afterwards by services to Elkhart, Indiana. As traffic grew, the original Doves were succeeded by Beech 99 and Twin Otter turboprops, and it was later decided to standardise on the Swearingen Metro for the 16-seater size of aircraft. By 1979, a total of 14 Metro IIs were in service on routes serving Wisconsin, Michigan, Illinois, Indiana, Ohio, Nebraska and Minnesota, and the following year the first of 10 50-passenger DH-C Dash-7s entered service. The average stage length of the network, which extended as far east as Pittsburgh, Pennsylvania, was now 145 miles and

five major traffic hubs were served, a large proportion of passengers interlining to catch domestic trunk or international flights.

What had attracted Air Wisconsin to the 146 were two features in particular: its quietness and its low fuel burn. The Metro carried 16 passengers at about 260mph and used just over 100gal/hr; the 50-passenger Dash-7 at the same speed burnt almost 290gal/hr, whereas the 109-passenger 146s consumed not much more than 600US gal/hr in service, even though for air traffic control reasons they rarely got above 17,000ft and spent a good deal of their time in the Chicago terminal area. Air Wisconsin's main base was at Outagamie Airport, Appleton, but new maintenance facilities for the 146 were built at Fort Wayne, Indiana, these calling for an extra 150 staff to bring the airline's total to over 600. So taken was Air Wisconsin's president, Preston Wilbourne, with the 146, that he acquired the registration BAE146 for his car number plate.

The first 146, N601AW, went straight into a gruelling 13 scheduled flights a day timetable, serving Chicago O'Hare Airport five times a day, and being a frequent visitor to Appleton, Toledo (Ohio) and Fort Wayne. Its wide cabin proved to be popular with passengers and the 146s generated new traffic, so that Air Wisconsin carried 44% more passengers in December 1983 than in the corresponding month of 1982. By early 1984, schedules called for 59 landings a day by the four 146s in service, only the limitations of slot times at Chicago O'Hare preventing an even higher total; there was no preferential treatment for the 146 at O'Hare. Average sector length flown by the 146s was 127 miles. Productivity of the 146 in terms of seat-miles proved to be better than expected; it had been assumed that a 146 would be worth the seat-mile capacity of two Dash-7s, but it turned out to be worth three, and the 146's fuel burn per seat-mile proved to be fractionally less than the Dash-7's. This enabled the latter to be displaced from a number of routes, and finally sold off, as were the Metros.

As traffic grew, a repeat order was placed early in 1984 for two more 146s plus two more on option, the first of these, N605AW, leaving Hatfield on delivery on 21 July 1984, followed by N606AW *Kitty* (named after the president's wife), which entered service on 1 March 1985. With five 146s in service, the airline was achieving a utilisation of 4.78hr daily for each aircraft at the end of July 1984, and a typical turn-round time on the ground was a mere 12min. Both 146 passenger entrance doors have built-in airstairs, and passengers disembarking from the forward door are accelerated down the aisle by passengers embarking from the rear. Profitability was ensured by actual passenger load factors averaging about 47%, while break-even load factor was a mere 36%.

Traffic growth led to an earlier option for a seventh 146 being taken up, this, registered N607AW, being handed over at Hatfield on 15 January 1986, and an eighth, N608AW, left Hatfield on delivery on 24 April that year. A point of interest is that these were the first two 146s to have Class B test registrations applied for pre-delivery test flying, a practice that was to become standard for most 146s delivered subsequently. N607AW had first flown as G-5-001 and N608AW as G-5-002, although normally the last three numbers of the Class B registration were the same as the 146's constructor's number, N610AW, the 10th, which first flew as G-5-08, having the constructor's number E.2082; this left Hatfield on delivery on 16 September 1987. The 9th, N609AW, had been registered as G-BNKK to BAe for display at the 1987 Paris Salon, leaving on its delivery flight after the show on 19 June. By now traffic growth had justified an order announced the previous month for five of the stretched 146 Series 300s, and with the delivery of the first two of these at the end of 1988 two of the first Series 200s were withdrawn from service; N603AW was traded in to BAe, being delivered to Hatfield on 9 January 1989, and later went to the Leeds/Bradford-based commuter operator Capital Airlines as

G-OSKI. N604AW was leased by BAe to the Canadian operator Air Nova as G-FEXN from 11 June 1989, and later went to Capital as G-OSUN.

When Air Wisconsin first started operations in 1965 it was, like others of its kind, classed as a scheduled air taxi operator by the FAA, although these were more popularly known as commuter airlines or third level operators. The latter term denoted a third level of service to the smaller communities and 'one-horse towns', below the second level of the local service airlines and the first level of the major domestic trunk carriers. By 1978, when the US Airline Deregulation Act came into force, there were 228 commuter airlines in the States with a total of 1,047 aircraft; average number of seats per aircraft was 12. Increasingly, during the 1980s the term 'regional airlines' superseded 'commuter airlines', so much so that in 1981 the Commuter Airline Association of America changed its title to the Regional Airline Association (RAA), and operators like Air Wisconsin were known as regionals for short.

Deregulation brought drastic changes to the regionals; in particular the advent of computerised reservations systems (or CRS) for the major domestic airlines meant that regional airlines entered code-sharing agreements with the former to enable their flights to be listed in the major's CRS system under its own code. Indeed, without such an agreement with a major carrier, a regional airline has little chance of survival on its own, at least in the States. With the advent of CRS systems, the hub-and-spoke concept was developed in which as much traffic as possible was funnelled into big city hub airports like Chicago or Dallas by the regionals and this led to their being much more closely integrated with,

Below:
Aspen Airways' 146 Series 200, N463AP, in the United Express livery also worn by 146s of Air Wisconsin and WestAir Commuter Airlines; Aspen became a United Express operator on 1 September 1986.

and tightly controlled by, the major domestic carriers. The latter stepped up the assistance they furnished to the regionals (and hence the control they could exert over them), providing marketing assistance, financial assistance for new aircraft — or even, in some cases, doing all of a regional's accounting for it. Some of the latter (but not Air Wisconsin) became wholly-owned subsidiaries of a major domestic carrier, for all practical purposes part of it although operating under their own names.

This resulted in several groups of regional airlines each flying for a major domestic carrier under a 'brand name' such as American Eagle, Continental Express, Pan Am Express or United Express, with its aircraft restyled in the same basic livery as the major carrier. So it was that Air Wisconsin, on 26 October 1986, became part of the United Express group of regionals, flying services into Chicago O'Hare for United Airlines and also moving out of its traditional midwestern states operating area to provide services into United's hub at Washington Dulles Airport and six other cities in the eastern part of the USA.

Early in 1988 another BAe146 operator, Presidential Airways Inc, which had just joined the United Express group, took over responsibility for all its services into the Washington Dulles hub, leaving Air Wisconsin to concentrate on its traditional hub at Chicago O'Hare, which was also the focal point of the whole United Airlines network. After its redeployment from Washington Dulles, Air Wisconsin opened up new routes from Chicago to the southeastern states, serving Lexington (Kentucky), Charleston (West Virginia) and Roanoke (Virginia), all with three round trips daily. By the summer of 1988, it was possible to fly right across the USA by the 146s of four regionals, all part of United Express: these were Westair Commuter Airlines of Fresno, California, Aspen Airways of Denver, Colorado, Air Wisconsin and Presidential Airways.

Air Wisconsin's orders for the 146 Series 200 had placed the sales emphasis firmly on the larger version of the 146, and BAe Hatfield's original expectations of 1973-74 that the Series 100 would account for about two-thirds of total sales proved in the end to be unfounded. This emphasis was strengthened even further by the joint announcement in San Diego, California, and London on 16 November 1983, of an order for 20 146 Series 200s plus 25 on option from Pacific Southwest Airlines Inc — PSA, of San Diego, the major Californian inter-state carrier; this order was valued at an initial $300 million and called for the delivery of the first eight 146s during 1984 and the remaining 12 in 1985. This was the largest single order to be placed for the 146 and possibly the most significant of all, since PSA operated high-frequency low-fare services in the intensely competitive Californian markets and to neighbouring states. By the time its 146 order was placed, it had grown to be one of the largest truly short-haul airlines in the world. At the time its 146 order was announced, PSA was operating some 325 flights daily over a route network serving 19 cities in California, Oregon, Washington, Nevada, Arizona and New Mexico. Most important of these routes were those between San Diego, Los Angeles and San Francisco, high-frequency shuttle services being operated between these cities in what was known as the Californian Corridor. The San Francisco-Los Angeles route is one of the busiest domestic air routes in the world.

As an intra-state airline operating within the borders of California, PSA's fares were regulated and approved by the California Public Utilities Commission, and not by the Civil Aeronautics Board — CAB, and this has enabled PSA to offer fares around 20% lower than those of competing interstate airlines like TWA and United. This has been a major factor in PSA's growth, as a combination of low fares and high-frequency with no frills on Californian Corridor routes has proved over the years to be a powerful attraction.

PSA was formed to operate scheduled services in California as the airline division of Friedkin Aeronautics Inc of San Diego, which had started in 1945; PSA began services on 6 May 1949 with a weekly return flight from San Diego to San Francisco/Oakland via Burbank using a leased DC-3. A second DC-3 entered service at the end of 1949 and by 1952 four of these were being operated; in November 1955 the first two 70-seat DC-4s started operations, followed by two more later. In November 1959, the first of six Lockheed Electra turboprops seating 98 passengers joined the fleet and, with these, high-frequency shuttle services between San Francisco, Los Angeles and San Diego were developed.

PSA now really began to grow, with the first Boeing 727-14 entering service in June 1965, followed at the end of 1967 by the first 727-214 and the first Boeing 737 on 20 September 1968; the airline was by now all-jet, although the 737s were later sold. The first of two 296-passenger Lockheed L-1011 TriStars was delivered on 2 July 1974, but a combination of the post-1973 economic recession and restrictive fuel quotas prevented them from being used to full advantage and they were eventually returned to Lockheed. In the struggle to dominate the highly competitive San Francisco-Los Angeles routes, PSA's passenger carryings had increased from

Left:
Pacific Southwest Airlines' order of November 1983 for 20 146 Series 200s, plus 25 on option, was the largest and one of the most important to be placed for the type. PSA's first 146, N346PS, seen here, flew the airline's first service with the type from Burbank to Oakland, on 20 June 1984; note the PSA 'smile' on the nose.

over 3 million in 1967 to more than 8 million in 1983. The 727s and 737s enabled more places to be added to the network, and at one time there were more than 30 727s in the fleet. But by the time of PSA's 146 order, only eight 727-200s were left, plus 24 McDonnell Douglas DC-9 Super 80s (or MD-80s) and four DC-9 Series 30s.

Whereas Air Wisconsin, in choosing the 146, had moved up in size from its 50-passenger DHC Dash-7s, a striking feature of PSA's 146 order was that it represented a trading down in size from the 727s and the 150-passenger MD-80s to the 100-passenger 146; in other words trading size for higher frequency of service. This policy was necessary because deregulation had meant more intense competition, more airlines entering the market and hence declining traffic shares. In fact the eight 727-200s were to be phased out as 146s were delivered as they used twice the amount of fuel as a 146 and would not have met the more stringent Federal Aviation Administration noise regulations that were to become effective in 1985. The 146's quietness was also a major selling point in winning the PSA order, enabling it to operate into some of the USA's most noise-sensitive airports such as Burbank and John Wayne Airport serving Orange County. The first 146s were to be deployed on PSA's lower-density routes initially; PSA's average sector length was 370 miles and flying time one hour.

As Mr Paul C. Barkley, PSA's President and Chief Operating Officer, said in explaining his choice of the 146, the aircraft would offer trip costs some 30% less than those achieved by the MD-80s. 'The 146 can provide a higher frequency without increasing costs and a lower cost when no more than 100 seats are needed' he added.

He felt that the 146 offered versatility coupled with the ability to provide frequency and efficiency in less-dense markets. It would make possible more direct services between smaller cities where traffic densities would not be attractive to bigger carriers with larger aircraft. Finally the 146 would be able to provide back-up services to the MD-80s in high-density high-frequency markets during off-peak times.

Pending delivery of its first aircraft, PSA borrowed Air Wisconsin's third 146 Series 200, N603AW, to demonstrate over its routes and for noise measurement tests at Burbank and San Jose, both places with strong environmental lobbies against noise. Decibel readings noted on take-off from Burbank included an MD-80 at 97.6dB, a Boeing 727 at 106dB and the 146 at 82.3dB; an increase of 10dB doubles the noise heard on the ground. At San Jose noise measurements showed the 146 to be significantly quieter than a Sabreliner executive jet, consecutive take-offs giving a reading of 72.5dB for the 146 against 90.3dB for the Sabreliner. One one take-off when the 146 turned during the initial climb no reading was obtained at the usual monitoring position, and the 146 left no measurable trace during a level flypast at 500ft. There was extensive TV coverage of these demonstrations, which showed that environmentalists were convinced that PSA had made the right choice with the 146.

PSA's first 146, N346PS, was handed over at Hatfield on 30 May 1984 and left on its delivery flight on 13 June, flying PSA's first service with the type, from Burbank to Oakland, on 20 June. In the meantime, the second 146 Series 100, G-SSHH, now re-registered G-OPSA in honour of its newest customer, had left Hatfield on 17 March for a demonstration tour of the States and for lease to PSA for crew training pending delivery of their first few 146s. It was fitted out to seat 74 passengers and had a larger than usual forward galley, as well as provision for carrying the large amount of sales brochures and other promotional literature necessary during a sales tour. It visited both the Avco plants participating in the 146 programme — Avco Lycoming at Stratford, Connecticut, where ALF 502s were built, and Avco Aerostructures at Nashville, Tennessee, where 146 wings are made, so giving Avco employees at both plants their first sight of the 146.

In a 16-day journey G-OPSA also called at New York, Washington Dulles, Miami, Denver and Phoenix, Arizona, arriving at San Diego on 4 April for a spell of crew training with PSA. It returned to Chester on 17 June and left Hatfield on 10 July on another demonstration tour, to the Far East, and after this was completed it was leased again to PSA as N5828B for another spell from 12 October to the following March. Conversion time for PSA's 64 flightdeck crews at San Diego during the first spell of training averaged less than 10hr.

By the end of 1984 PSA had six 146s in service, and all 20 were painted with a smile on their noses (a practice that had started with the TriStars), being known as 'Smile Liners'. During 1986 they were given names linking this 'service with a smile' concept to places in the States that they served; thus N346PS was named 'The Smile of Medford' and later 'The Smile of PSA', N347PS became 'The Smile of Tri-Cities' and so on through the fleet of 20, which were registered N346PS to N365PS. By the end of July 1984 the first three 146s had completed 590 flights since the inaugural on 20 June; utilisation was building up to a daily target of 11hr and a 97% on-time departure record had already been established. With a fuel burn no less than 37% lower than that of PSA's MD-80s and comparable seat-mile costs, the 146s were well suited to maintaining PSA's competitive position on the Californian Corridor routes.

Last of the order for 20 was N365PS which left Hatfield on delivery on 19 December 1985, and PSA's 146s were then achieving a daily utilisation of 9.2hr (shortly to be increased to 10.5hr) with an average of 183 departures a day being scheduled. Options on four more were taken up early in 1986 from the 25 on option with the original order; of these four, N366PS to N369PS,

the first three were delivered in June 1987 and the fourth in July. All four were registered to US Air Leasing & Services Inc in June 1987. N366PS was registered G-BNJI in April 1987 for demonstrations and visited London Heathrow on 6 May carrying the President of Mozambique. N368PS was briefly registered G-BNND in June 1987 before delivery to PSA; at the end of 1988 it was returned to BAe and leased to Air UK as G-BNND from 15 December to 12 March 1989. N369PS was sold to the Danish airline Cimber Air as OY-CRG for use by the new Faroe Islands carrier Atlantic Airways, for whom it flew the first service on 28 March 1988 from Vagar to Copenhagen. Also, N359PS had been registered to BAe as G-BMFM just before delivery, for demonstrations at Nice from 30 September to 3 October 1985. Two 146s were leased to provide extra capacity at various times, the ex-Air Pac N146AP for six months from 15 December 1986, and 146 Series 100 N246SS (formerly G-SSCH, the third development aircraft) returned from its spell with the short-lived British Caribbean Airways for lease to PSA from 13 November 1986 to 19 September the following year.

The mid-1980s saw a spate of airline mergers in the USA, where domestic air transport became increasingly polarised between the very big and very small airlines, not always to the passengers' advantage. As Regional Airline Association president Michael Boyd observed during 1987, deregulation had failed under what he termed 'poor decision making and questionable leadership at the Department of Transportation' in allowing the mergers of TWA and Ozark Airlines and Northwest Orient and Republic, which created such a dominant position at airport hubs as to preclude free market entry — one of the basic principles of deregulation. 'The vertical integration of the airline system from commuter level to 747s, plus the lack of meaningful government control over mergers, means that there is little or no chance for additional new jet carriers to compete in the marketplace in any meaningful way' said Mr Boyd, adding 'the environment has been redesigned to effectively keep new competition out'.

As part of this process USAir Group Inc, the parent company of Washington, DC-based USAir, formerly Allegheny Airlines and one of the major local service carriers in the USA, which had grown to serve nearly 100 cities in 31 states, the District of Columbia and two Canadian provinces, announced plans to purchase Pacific Southwest in December 1986 as well as the North Carolina-based Piedmont Airlines, another major local service airline. By 1988, Piedmont had grown to serve 122 cities in 30 states and the District of Columbia, and had several international routes, including a newly-opened one to London (Gatwick), as well as others to Ottawa and Montreal and to Nassau in the Bahamas. The USAir Group acquired Pacific Southwest on 29 May 1987 at a cost of $385 million, and PSA's operations were to be merged into USAir by April 1988; USAir then operated 147 aircraft, including Boeing 737-300s, 737-200s, 727-200s, DC-9 Series 30s and One-Eleven 200s, and the combined USAir/PSA fleet exceeded 200 aircraft. With the USAir purchase of Piedmont for $1.6 billion in 1987, the resulting airline had over 420 aircraft and more than 43,000 employees. PSA was officially merged into USAir on 9 April 1988, and integrated schedules were due to begin on 2 May. The 146s had been re-registered from November 1987 to reflect USAir ownership, N346PS to N369PS being re-registered (respectively) N163US, N165US to N168US, N171US to N175US, N177US to N179US, N181US, N183US to N185US, and N187US to N193US.

The first fatal, accident involving a 146 occurred on 8 December 1987 when N350PS was on flight PS1771 from Los Angeles to San Francisco. David Burke, aged 34, a sacked PSA worker with a grudge, smuggled a gun aboard the flight to kill the man who had sacked him for stealing, Mr Ray Thompson, USAir's customer services manager at Los Angeles, who was a passenger. Having shot him, Burke then apparently made his way into the cockpit and shot the two pilots — ballistic tests on his gun, which was recovered from the wreckage, showed that it had fired six bullets. The 146's flight recorder revealed 'a terrible commotion' on the flightdeck and the scream of engines as it dived towards the ground, out of control. It crashed into woods near Paso Robles, California, killing all 43 people on board; the wreckage was spread over a 15-mile area.

Just as sad in its own way was the disappearance with the USAir takeover of the low fares which PSA had brought the Californian travelling public and which had contributed so powerfully to its own growth. In an article in the Los Angeles Times of mid-1989 about California's airlines after deregulation, Robert A. Jones wrote of the PSA takeover; 'When PSA turned the keys over, it was charging $140 for a full-fare, round-trip ticket between LA and San Francisco. Today USAir charges $296 for the same ticket. So does American, so does United, so do they all. In the space of the 15 months since the majors took over the California market, they have doubled the fares . . . I remember, in the 1960s, there was a way to fly on PSA that

seemed cheaper than hitch-hiking. If you were young, or sufficiently desperate, all you needed to do was to show up at 11.55pm and catch PSA's Midnight Flyer. No reservations, no meals, no assigned seat. The charge was $10. What few of us realised was the fragility of it all.'

In February 1991, as part of a major cost-cutting and restructuring operation begaun after a net loss of $454 million was posted for 1990, USAir announced its decision to sell the 18 BAe 146s remaining from the 24 it had inherited with the takeover of PSA, citing what it claimed were 'the type's high operating costs' in the ultra-competitive Californian Corridor markets. The entry of several new operators such as Delta, Alaskan, America West and Northwest Orient into these markets since the PSA takeover had increased competition, especially on the Los Angeles-San Francisco shuttle route, and fares had been cut. PSA had reduced the seating capacity of its 146s from the original 100 to 81 after passengers had complained about lack of room in the window seats and this, claimed UAir, ' . . . put the operating economics of the aeroplane into a cocked hat'; the type was withdrawn from service by 2 May and replaced on some routes by Boeing 737-300s and '-400s and Fokker 100s, and services to six Californian cities were dropped entirely. But of the eight USAir routes in California neighbouring states from which the airline withdrew, only four were 146 routes.

But BAe was annoyed at what it saw as USAir's attempt to cast the 146 in the role of scapegoat for its cutbacks, and issued a rebuttal of some of the airline's claims, pointing out that the 146 fleet had been the fundamental and key element of the whole PSA — and later USAir — California route strategy. Reduction of the seating to 85 five-abreast was partly to give passengers more room after some complaints about the previous six-abreast layout but also to introduce a small first-class section. BAe also pointed out that air fares in the Los Angeles-San Francisco corridor were now as low as $20 one way for a distance of 339 miles, compared with $178 for the 184-mile long New York-Boston route. USAir's 146s, just before their withdrawal, were recording the lowest delay and highest despatch reliability rate (99.1%) of any of the 446 airliners operated by the airline. USAir withdrew its criticisms of the 146, saying 'It is not the aircraft's fault. It is the marketing conditions which are behind our decision. You have got low fare carriers who are determined to beat each others' brains out'. Fare-cutting and ultra-keen competition had effectively prevented the 146's continued operation in the California markets and USAir had no other routes to run them on. Also

figures filed with the US Department of Transportation had shown a decreasing market share for USAir in California, forcing down fares so that revenue yields were substantially lower than on the rest of the USAir network, and break-even load factors almost twice as high. Again, the airline's engine maintenance costs, both for the 146's ALF 502s and the Pratt & Whitney JT8Ds of the 737-200 fleet, were much higher than those of other major US airlines.

Next US customer to add 146s to its fleet was Aspen Airways Inc of Denver, Colorado, which served the well known ski resort of Aspen in Colorado as well as Colorado Springs and Durango in that state, and other places in New Mexico, Texas, Utah, Wyoming and Iowa. Aspen Airways was formed as an air taxi operator in 1953 and became an FAA Part I21 certificated operator in 1967. It ordered two 146 Series 100s to supplement its existing fleet of 10 Convair 580 turboprops, and the first of these, N461AP (previously G-5-01) was handed over at Hatfield on 6 December 1984, and entered service between Denver and Aspen on Boxing Day that year, at the height of the skiing season. The second 146, N462AP, left Chester

on delivery on 7 June 1985, and had first worn the test registration G-5-02 for two development flights, and had then become G-BLRA for a period of crew training. Aspen became a United Express carrier on 1 September 1986 following the signing of a agreement to operate services into United's Denver hub, and a third 146 Series 100 was ordered. This, N463AP, was delivered on 18 December 1986 and a fourth 146, N246SS, the former G-SSCH, the third development aircraft, which had been operated for a few months by British Caribbean Airways before being leased to Pacific Southwest, was leased from the Tracy Leasing Corp in December 1987, being purchased outright a few months later. This enabled several new places to be added to the network, which now extended into Montana and North and South Dakota, covering 16 cities. Late in 1989 Aspen Airways was sold to the Giant Group, a manufacturer whose activities ranged from cement to recycled newsprint.

The 146 In Australia
The first Australian order for the 146, from Ansett Transport Industries for its wholly-owned subsidiary Airlines of Western Australia, although

for only two 146 Series 200s, was an important order. It marked the return of a major British airliner into the mainstream of Australian air transport after two decades of that country operating mainly Boeing, McDonnell Douglas and Fokker types. It was also particularly gratifying for BAe since Airlines of Western Australia, at the time of the 146 order, was equipped wholly with the 146's main commercial rival, the Fokker F28, operating two F28-4000s and six F28-1000s, and under its previous name of MacRobertson Miller Airline Services — MMA, it had flown Fokker F27 Friendships since December 1959.

MMA had its origins in the Commercial Aviation Co formed by Capt H. C. Miller in 1919 for joy-riding, air taxi work and charters. In 1927 it started scheduled services from Adelaide and that year with the support, mainly financial, of Sir MacPherson Robertson, the confectionery magnate (who put up the prize money for the famous MacRobertson Trophy Race of 1934), the airline became the MacRobertson Miller Aviation Co Pty Ltd. In April 1934 MMA was awarded the contract to carry airmail over the 2,252-mile route from Perth up the Western Australian coast to Daly Waters, this route (which in August 1938 was extended to Darwin) linking up with the Qantas/Imperial Airways services to London. This same basic route is the backbone of Airlines of Western Australia's system and it is now flown by the 146s; MMA started operating it with three DH84 Dragons which in 1938 were replaced by two DH86 Express four-engined biplanes. MMA merged with another Perth-based operator, Airlines (WA) Ltd, with effect from 1 October 1955; Airlines (WA) served Kalgoorlie and the goldfield regions of Western Australia. Ansett Transport Industries acquired a 68% interest in MMA in April 1963 and bought up the remaining 32% in January 1969; on 1 July 1981 MMA was renamed Airlines of Western Australia.

The first 146, VH-JJP, left Hatfield on delivery on 22 April 1985 and flew its first service, from Perth to the gold-mining town of Kalgoorlie, on 28 June. It was soon followed by VH-JJQ, which left Hatfield on delivery on 22 June; the 'JJ' in their registrations derives from the 146's Australian nickname of 'Junior Jumbo'. Airlines of Western Australia had been renamed Ansett WA in December 1984, and a third 146 was ordered at the end of 1987 plus two more early in 1988; these were delivered as VH-JJS, VH-JJT and VH-JJW in (respectively) October and November 1988 and March 1989. The network now extends to Ayers Rock and Alice Springs in the Northern Territory as well as serving the coastal regions from Perth to Darwin and Kunumurra..

The Ansett Transport Industries group was to become one of the largest 146 customers, for its subsidiary — Ansett New Zealand — ordered two 146 Series 200s on 14 October 1988 and five Series 300s the following January for its domestic routes, which link Auckland, Wellington, Christchurch, Dunedin, Rotorua, Mount Cook and Queenstown. The first of the two Series 200s, ZK-NZA, was delivered on 15 July 1989 followed soon after by ZK-NZB; these each seat 75 passengers. The airline has announced plans to standardise on the 146 for its jet equipment and to dispose of its current Boeing 737-100s and -200s; it will not now proceed with its planned purchase of twin jets. Coming from such an important customer as the Ansett group this endorsement of the 146 is indeed gratifying. In addition to Ansett New Zealand another subsidiary, Ansett Air Freight, has two 146 Series 200QT freighters on order for it and this variant is the subject of a major commitment for up to 72 aircraft by the TNT Group (Thomas Nationwide Transport), co-owner of Ansett Transport Industries, of which firm orders have now been placed for 23, as related in Chapter 7. In addition,

Left:
Handover ceremony of the first 146 CC Mk 2 for the Queen's Flight, ZE700, at Hatfield on 23 April 1986; British Aerospace chairman Sir Austin Pearce handed over the aircraft's logbook to Air Vice-Marshal John Severne, Captain of the Queen's Flight.

East-West Airlines of New South Wales, the first operator to declare publicly its interest in the 146 before the first flight, and which has eight Series 300s on order, became part of the Ansett group in 1987.

Queen's Flight and Other VIP 146s

Following the successful evaluation of the fourth and fifth development 146 Series 100s in service with No 10 Squadron at Brize Norton as (respectively) ZD695 and ZD696 (as related in Chapter 3), an order for two 146 Series 200s for the Queen's Flight was announced on 1 August 1984. They were to be known as BAe146 CC Mk 2s to distinguish them from the earlier Series 100s, which were BAe146 C Mk 1s. The two latter had flown over 800hr in RAF service. The first CC Mk 2, ZE700 (formerly G-5-02), was handed over at Hatfield on 23 April 1986, in a ceremony in which its logbook was handed over by Sir Austin Pearce, BAe chairman, to AVM John Severne, Captain of the Queen's Flight. ZE700 was delivered to RAF Benson, home of the Queen's Flight, on 6 May and was followed by the second CC Mk 2, ZE701 (ex-G-5-03), on 9 July. Both of them had the optional wing root fuel tanks for greater range. They were painted in an attractive all-white colour scheme with a dark blue fuselage flash and red wings and tailplane, with wing and tailplane leading edges, ailerons and elevators in natural aluminium.

First use of a CC Mk 2 in Queen's Flight service came on 23 July 1986 when ZE700 flew the newly-married Duke and Duchess of York from London Heathrow to the Azores on the first stage of their honeymoon; inside one of the rear fuselage air brakes a plate had been fitted bearing the words 'JUST MARRIED'! Later, when the Duchess of York used one of the 146s to fly to a skiing holiday at Meribel in the French Alps on 31 January 1988, it was seen to be fitted with a chaff or flare dispenser in a bulge under the fuselage, just aft of the rear airstairs, to confuse heat-seeking missiles that might be launched by terrorist groups; two small ventral underfins were also fitted housing electronic sensors to warn of such missiles. Similar devices had also been fitted to the Lockheed TriStars and VC10s used by the Royal Family and the Prime Minister. Among the places visited by the 146 CC Mk 2s in the course of official business have been Costa Rica, Belize, Mexico and Ascension Island. An order for a third 146 CC Mk 2 for the Queen's Flight was announced in October 1989. This, serialled ZE702, was handed over to HM the Queen at RAF Benson on 21 December 1990. By this time the first two had flown over 2 million miles and 5,200 hours.

Announced on the same day as the handover of the first 146 CC Mk 2 for the Queen's Flight was the BAe 146 Statesman, a new executive version of the 146 suitable for the use of a President or head of state, and based on the experience gained in preparing the 146s for Royal service. The Statesman would be available in Series 100 or 200 form with an executive/VIP interior featuring various combinations of state rooms, conference rooms and staff quarters, with additional galley and wardrobe space provided as required, the interior making the best use of the 146's large cabin volume. The 146's ability to operate into short gravel strips, from airports close to townships and from mountain-locked runways, offered maximum flexibility in planning presidential visits, while optional wing root fuel tanks enable the operational range for such visits to be extended from 1,400nm to 1,600nm.

The first 146 to be completed to Statesman standard was Series 200 PK-PJP (formerly G-5-517 and G-5-004), to be operated as a Presidential and VIP transport for the Indonesian Government by Pelita Air Service (Pertambangan Minjak National), which was the aviation division of Indonesia's state oil company Pertamina, which undertakes a wide variety of services, especially in support of oilfield and natural gas exploitation. Pelita operates over 40 fixed-wing aircraft, ranging from L-100-30 Hercules and Transall C-160 freighters to executive jets, and its fleet of about 60 helicopters are used extensively on oil drilling rig support and related oil and gas operations.

The first export 146 had gone to Mali for the use of that country's President and government ministers, and also the national airline, Air Mali. Zimbabwe was the second African country to follow this example of joint use by the government for VIP transport and the national airline, when a 146 Series 200 was ordered by the Government of Zimbabwe for its own use and also that of Air Zimbabwe. This first flew as G-5-065 on 18 December 1986, later acquiring the Zimbabwe registration Z-WPD, and it left Hatfield on delivery through Athens on 29 November 1987. The latest government to acquire a 146 is that of the United Arab Emirates, for whom Series 100 Statesman A6-SHK, left Hatfield on delivery via Rhodes on 20 December 1988; this had first flown as G-5-091 and had then become G-BOMA of BAe. It was flown to Basle in Switzerland on 2 June 1988 for fitting out with a VIP interior by Jet Aviation AG; this features quickly variable seating capacity in the VIP and business-class sections, the VIP part of the cabin seating from 10 to 18 while the business class (or staff transport) section can be reduced from 44 to 29 seats.

China's Choice

As mentioned previously, the second development 146 Series 100, G-OPSA (formerly G-SSHH), after a spell on lease to PSA for crew training following a demonstration tour of the States, had returned to Chester on 17 June 1984 and had left Hatfield on 10 July on another sales tour, this time to the Far East, arriving at Hong Kong on the 13th and departing for Peking (now Beijing) two days later for demonstrations to China's national airline CAAC (the Civil Aviation Administration of China). The 146 spent 14 days in mainland China travelling more widely in that country than any foreign aircraft had ever done before, and visiting 13 airfields, many of which had never witnessed a non-Chinese aircraft on the ramp before. Among the high spots of the tour (literally, as well as figuratively) was a landing at Lhasa, Tibet, which has the highest airport in the world at an altitude of some 16,000ft, while landings made at the Chinese coastal town of Zhangjiang confirmed once again the 146's ability to operate from short, narrow runways. The 146 carried a permanent team of six CAAC personnel throughout its journeyings, and altogether some 600 Chinese people flew in it.

The 146 returned to Hong Kong on 28 July and continued on through Korea, Japan, Brunei, Indonesia and Singapore before leaving for home via Nepal, where a landing was made at another high altitude airport, that serving the capital of Kathmandu at 4,386ft above sea level; further stops were made in India, Pakistan, Bahrain and Cyprus before the 146 arrived back at Hatfield on 17 August at the end of a 40,000-mile tour covering 17 countries in all. After leaving China, a

Left:
On the roof of the world. The second 146 Series 100, G-OPSA (formerly G-SSHH), is refuelled at the Tibetan capital Lhasa's airport, which is the highest in the world at some 16,000ft, during its sales and demonstration tour of China in July 1984. To the left is a Boeing 707-3J6B or '-3J6C of the Chinese state airline CAAC.

Right:
The sales tour of China led to an order for 10 146 Series 100s for CAAC, of which the first is seen here wearing its Class B test registration G-5-019. After appearing at the 1986 Farnborough display as G-XIAN it was delivered as B-2701 to its Chinese base of Lanzhou on 14 September 1986.

further 700 people representing airlines and other interested parties had sampled a flight in the 146, and all the flights programmed before leaving the UK had been completed on time. In 120hr of flying, a total of 113 landings had been made at a wide variety of airfields — hot, high, short and rough — and the 146 had displayed exceptional reliability and low fuel consumption. After its Far East tour, G-OPSA went to Pacific SouthWest for another spell on lease, this time as N5828B, from 12 October 1984 to the following March.

The 146's exceptional performance on its extensive tour of China soon bore fruit in the shape of a memorandum of understanding signed by the Chinese Government for the purchase of 10 146 Series 100s for delivery, beginning in June 1986. This memorandum of understanding was converted into a firm contract worth $150 million and signed at Beijing on 28 May 1985. The contract was negotiated with the China Aviation Supplies Corp — CASC. China was no stranger to British aircraft, as CAAC had taken delivery of six Viscount 843s (the last of this type to be built), the first Viscount service, between Peking and Shanghai, being flown on 25 March 1964. Four surplus Trident 1Es were acquired from Pakistan International Airlines in 1970 and experience with these led to orders for a total of 33 Trident 2Es from CAAC plus two Super Trident 3Bs, the first Trident 2E being delivered in November 1972. Tridents supplemented CAAC's other types on major inter-city routes such as Peking-Canton and Peking-Shanghai, and 21 of the Mk 2Es and the two Super Trident 3Bs were still in service in 1990.

The first three 146s were to be based in Lanzhou in the Central Uplands, administered by the regional headquarters of Xian, and to fly services from Lanzhou to Chengdu and the Tibetan capital of Lhasa. The next three 146s were to be based in the Shanghai region and the last four at Hohhot in the Beijing region. The first CAAC 146 had made its maiden flight as G-5-019 on 7 April 1986 and was briefly G-5-523 before reverting to the original Class B registration; it became G-XIAN for the 1986 SBAC Display at Farnborough, being handed over at the show on 2 September and taking part in the flying display, flying in the BAe formation of two 146s, a BAe125 executive jet and a Jetstream 31. It left Hatfield on delivery in its Chinese registration B-2701 on 10 September, arriving at its home base of Lanzhou on the 14th. The remaining aircraft, B-2702 to B-2710, followed at roughly monthly intervals, the last one, B-2710, leaving Hatfield on delivery on 6 August 1987.

The 146s arrived at a time when CAAC was undergoing a major structural reorganisation which involved concentrating increasingly on its role as a regulatory body, and gradually reducing its airline operations by devolving them to a number of newly-formed regional airlines such as Xiamen Airlines based at Fujian, and China Southwest Airlines based at Chengdu. CAAC-Beijing, operating domestic and international routes from Beijing and including the 146s in its fleet, became known as Air China and from July 1988 operated all international services. The 146 order was part of a massive re-equipment programme in which Western types such as Boeing 747s, 757s, 767s and 737s, Airbus A310s and McDonnell Douglas MD-82s were ordered to supplement and eventually replace the now ageing Russian types such as Tu-154Ms, Il-18s and Antonov An-24s which had been dominant in the 1970s. In addition, a major airport construction programme is in hand, and the rapidly expanding domestic network numbers over 260 routes.

6 More Orders From America

With the 146 well established in service with Air Wisconsin and Pacific Southwest and achieving high utilisations, low fuel burns and an exceptionally low level of quietness with these carriers, it was not surprising that more regional airlines in the United States decided to feature the type in their re-equipment plans. Early in 1986 AirCal, known until April 1981 as Air California Inc, which operated high-frequency one-class services within California and also to Portland (Oregon), Seattle/Tacoma (Washington), Vancouver (British Columbia), Anchorage (Alaska) and Reno/Lake Tahoe (Nevada), ordered six 85-passenger 146 Series 200s. Two factors in particular lay behind AirCal's choice of the 146; it served many of the places in California that were on PSA's 146 routes, and the previous year a 146 Series 200

flown by a PSA crew had passed stringent noise limit tests to enable the type to be operated out of Orange County's John Wayne Airport, which was AirCal's base, without the reductions in passenger or fuel loads that other jets had to undergo in order to meet the airport's noise limits.

Since Orange County was one of the most noise-conscious communities in the States, the success of these 146 noise tests was of obvious importance to PSA and AirCal. For PSA to be allowed to operate 146 flights out of John Wayne Airport, the airline had to show that the 146 could take off at its maximum weight of 89,500lb without exceeding a noise limit of 98.5dB as it crossed a noise meter just after take-off; this was the most severe noise test to which the 146 had yet been subjected. As an added incentive, an airline was allowed to make two departures from

Left:
AirCal 146, N146AC, seen with BAe 125-800, G-BFAN, and one of the prototype 146s at a BAe Hatfield Open Day.

John Wayne Airport with a new type such as the 146, instead of one with older types such as 737s or DC-9s, provided that the new type did not exceed a single noise exposure of 89.5dB at any one of seven measuring points. The 146 was able to meet this challenge by such a wide margin that it could, if required, have carried a full load of 100 passengers and fuel from Orange County to Kansas City, 1,400 miles away, while still meeting the noise limitations. This would have allowed PSA freedom to schedule 146 flights 1,000 miles away to Seattle, at the northwestern limit of its existing route network.

Largely as a result of the 146 tests, John Wayne Airport increased its daily quota of jet departures from 41 to 55, and PSA was among the airlines that competed keenly for the additional slots. By contrast, other types were penalised by these noise limits; a Boeing 737-300 was unable to stay within the 89.5dB limit without a reduction in gross weight which left it able to carry only a 70% load — 100 passengers — from Orange County to the San Francisco Bay area, a distance of 372 miles. John Wayne Airport has a single runway only 5,700ft long, with some of the noise meters only 3,000ft from the runway's end in a residential area, yet from this runway the 146 Series 200 could lift a higher disposable load (payload plus fuel) than the Boeing 737-300, and the British type proved to have a 20% lower fuel consumption than the Boeing twinjet.

AirCal's first 146, N141AC, was handed over on 3 March 1986 and left Hatfield on delivery on the 5th, followed by the second, N142AC, on 22 March: these two inaugurated AirCal's first scheduled services with the type, between San Diego and Orange County's John Wayne Airport, on 1 April, although N142AC had been in service and operated an *ad hoc* charter on 25 March.

The remaining four 146s, N144AC, N145AC, N146AC and N148AC, followed soon after, the last of these, N148AC, being handed over at Hatfield on 26 September and leaving on delivery on 4 October 1986. The latter had first flown with the class B registration G-5-058 and was temporarily registered to BA as G-ECAL for display in the static park at the 1986 Farnborough show; it reverted to G-5-058 and was formally handed over to AirCal as such at Hatfield on 26 September, being delivered as N148AC.

At the same ceremony as the handing over of AirCal's last 146, the Queen's Award to Industry for Export Achievement of the BAe146 was presented by the Lord Lieutenant of Hertfordshire, Mr. S. Bowes Lyon, to Mr Sydney Gillibrand, Managing Director of BAe's Civil Aircraft Division. Receiving the Queen's Award, Mr Gillibrand recalled that seven airlines had placed orders for 27 BAe146s during 1985, the period covered by the award. All these were export orders and involved four United States airlines (including AirCal), operators in the Caribbean and South East Asia, as well as the China Aviation Supplies Corporation for CAAC. In 1985 the BAe146 had also gained the Technological Achievement Award, and AirCal's N148AC was the 50th export delivery.

Yet, barely a month after its delivery, AirCal had agreed to be taken over by American Airlines Inc; the formal takeover was completed on 30 April 1987 with AirCal's fleet (which also included nine Boeing 737-300s, 22 737-200s, two 737-100s and two McDonnell Douglas MD-80s as well as the 146s) was due to begin operating under AA flight codes from 1 July. Unlike other regional operators such as Command Airways and Simmons Airlines, which were also acquired by American but continued operating under their own names as wholly-owned subsidiaries under the American Eagle banner, AirCal did not survive its takeover by American as a separate entity. The 146s were taken over by American and from December 1988 were re-registered, N141AC and N142AC becoming N694AA and N695AA, and N144AC, N145AC, N146AC and N148AC becoming N696AA to N699AA. In November 1986 AirCal's parent company, AirCal Investments, or ACI Holdings, accepted an American Airlines bid of $15 a share for its 70% holding in AirCal, whose shares had been trading at $7. It was the latter's route network, especially within California, that was the main attraction for American, as it provided the presence on the US west coast and in the Californian markets that they needed.

Another airline whose BAe146 operations proved to be rather short-lived was British Caribbean Airways, based on Tortola in the British Virgin Islands, which ordered two 146 Series 100s early in 1986 to operate services direct and nonstop from Tortola to Miami. Tortola's limited runway length of 3,600ft prevented any other jet airliner from operating such services, but from it the 146 could lift a full load of 80 passengers at temperatures of up to 31°C. As the airline's managing director, Mr John Bull, explained: 'We are about to introduce

Below:
Royal West Airlines, the operating name of Aero West Inc, flew regional services from Las Vegas to California and neighbouring states with three 146 Series 100s, of which G-5-513 seen here was the former PT-LEQ of the Brazilian airline TABA, becoming N803RW in Royal West service.

something new and exciting into the Caribbean. Direct nonstop service into the British Virgin Islands from Miami in jet comfort has had to await the right aircraft. Now, with the BAe146 we can fly direct and nonstop between Miami and Tortola in less than three hours — avoiding the hassle of changing aircraft at San Juan (Puerto Rico) or St Thomas (in the US Virgin Islands) — and yet land on the short Beef Island runway.' The 146s were to seat 80 passengers and services were to begin on 17 April, subject to approvals being granted by both the United Kingdom and US governments. British Caribbean was registered in Tortola as a British Virgin Islands company, and management was provided on secondment from British Airways. Maintenance of its 146s was to be undertaken by Airtech Service of Miami, an FAA-approved service and overhaul centre for most current airliner types.

The third development 146 Series 100, G-SSCH, was earmarked for British Caribbean and, after a brief spell as G-5-14, was handed over on 17 March as N246SS. It left on delivery two days later, flying its first service on 17 April after making its first visit to Beef Island on a proving flight on 1 April. The second 146 was to have been the fourth development aircraft, originally G-SCHH, which after service with No 10 Squadron as ZD695 had been leased to Dan-Air as G-BRJS for six months in 1985; this was to have been N346SS in British Caribbean service, and was due for delivery in November. But the airline ceased operations on 12 October and N346SS was not delivered, having been held in storage in Chester without markings for some time; it was later leased to Dan-Air again as G-BRJS from 23 May to 7 June 1987. The first 146, N246SS, was flown to AAR Inc at Oklahoma City after British Caribbean's demise, and was then leased to Pacific Southwest for seven months from 13 November 1986.

Next 146 operator in the States was Royal West Airlines, the operating name of Aero West Inc of Las Vegas, Nevada, which began regional services with an initial fleet of three 146 Series 100s that had all been delivered in June 1986. First of these was the second development 146, G-OPSA (formerly G-SSHH), which had completed a sales tour of China and the Far East in 1984 in between spells on lease to PSA. Restored as G-SSHH, it had left Hatfield on 15 February 1986 on a demonstration tour to East Africa, returning 12 days later; it was painted in Royal West livery as N101RW, briefly becoming G-5-005 before leaving Hatfield on delivery on 9 June as N801RW. This was followed by the two former Brazilian 146s that had been operated by TABA, but had been grounded because the Brazilian government had insisted on such a high duty payment for spare parts. Of these, PT-LEP had become G-5-512 and left Hatfield for Reykjavik and demonstrations in the States as N802RW on 26 May, being officially handed over to Royal West on 18 June, and flying its first revenue service, to Los Angeles, on the 26th. PT-LEQ, now G-5-513, was handed over on 13 June and left Chester on delivery the following day as N803RW. All three were fitted out to accommodate 91 passengers and were planned to operate five return trips daily between Las Vegas and Los Angeles, five daily from Las Vegas to Burbank and two a day from Las Vegas to the Californian city of Ontario; there were also two daily return trips to Reno, Nevada, from Los Angeles and Las Vegas, and by the end of 1986 the 146s were flying 28-30 sectors per day over Royal West's routes.

The airline also developed block booking arrangements with tour operators in the region to take up a large portion of its available seats, although normal-category tickets at competitive fares were also very much on offer. During the 1986-87 winter sports season, Royal West's 146s began operating into the newly-built Eagle County Airport at Vail, Colorado, which offers access to the ski resort previously served only by Rocky Mountain Airways at the old Vail Airport. An order for several 146 Series 200s seemed likely, but this was not to be, for Royal West Airlines ceased scheduled operations on 27 February 1987 although some charter flights continued until 26 April.

Two of the 146s, N802RW and N803RW, remained in Royal West service a little longer, although nominally owned by the Tracey Lewasing Corp, and by October N802RW had been leased to another operator, Sunworld International Airways, as was N803RW, which flew its first service for Sunworld from Reno to Burbank on 1 December. However, Sunworld itself ceased operations on 14 January 1988, and N803RW was later returned to BAe Inc at Oklahoma City, and on 2 September went to Air Nova of Nova Scotia on lease as C-GNVY, as did its sister ship N802RW, which became C-GNVX. Sunworld International had been formed on 4 June 1981 as Jetwest International Airways, changing to its present name on 9 March 1982, and operated from Reno and Las Vegas to cities in California, Oregon, Washington, Idaho and to Oklahoma City and to Tucson (Arizona) with 737-300s and DC9s.

Royal West's first 146, N801RW, went to Dan-Air Services on lease as G-BPNP from 6 September to 10 November 1987, and then left Hatfield on 4 December on lease to American Eagle as N720BA, for use over the former AirCal

routes, flying its last service in this role from Santa Ana to Oakland on 14 February 1988. It was restored as G-BPNP and was at first earmarked for lease to Manx Airlines, but this plan was changed and instead it was modified into the prototype BAe146 STA military freighter, becoming G-BSTA.

Above:
Seen with air brakes out is N401XV, the first of eight 146 Series 200s for Presidential Airways Inc of Washington DC, the first 146 customer on the US east coast. N401XV was named *Franklin Pierce* and flew the first Presidential 146 service on 29 August 1986, just 10 weeks after the airline's order was announced.

Presidential Operations

First 146 customer on the US east coast was Presidential Airways Inc of Washington DC's Dulles International Airport, which in June 1986 ordered five 146 Series 200s with seven more on option to provide direct connections to Dulles International for communities too small to be served economically by Boeing 737-200s. Presidential had been formed in October 1985 by a group of former People Express executives, including Harold Pareti, the latter's former president, to operate high-frequency low-fare services into Washington's Dulles International Airport as a hub. Operations began on 10 October with 737-200 services to Boston (Mass), Hartford (Conn), Cincinatti (Ohio), Indianapolis (Indiana) and Miami (Fla). More cities in Florida were added to the network, as well as Cleveland (Ohio) and Montreal in Canada, and 12 737-200s were in use by May 1986. That same month, Presidential began to face a major competitive challenge when the giant United Airlines established a hub operation at Dulles International and, at the same time as the 146 order, a three-year joint marketing agreement with Pan-American was announced by Presidential to increase feeder traffic for the two airlines at Dulles and Miami.

The first 146, N401XV *Franklin Pierce*, was handed over to Presidential on 5 August 1986 and left Hatfield on delivery on the 8th; this flew the first Presidential 146 service on 29 August, a mere 10 weeks after the order had been announced. In receiving its log book at the handover ceremony, William D. Stockbridge, Presidential's Vice-President of Maintenance and Engineering, had noted the speed with which his airline and BAe had concluded their negotiations, thereby allowing a very rapid delivery of the first aircraft. The second 146, N402XV *James Buchanan,* left Hatfield on delivery on 28 August, and Presidential planned to use its 146s to increase frequency on its Dulles — New York (La Guardia) services, taking advantage of the aircraft's low noise signature to minimise environmental impact, As the 146 fleet built up, services to New York's John F. Kennedy International Airport and Washington National Airport were started, as well as to other cities among Presidential's 19 destinations served. The third 146, N403XV *Abraham Lincoln*, was registered to BAe as G-OHAP on 15 August to take part in the 1986 Farnborough Air Show; the registration reflected the initials of the airline's president, Harold Pareti, and this 146, after becoming briefly G-5-061, left Hatfield on delivery in its US registration on 13 September. It was followed by N404XV *Andrew Johnson* on 22 November, and N405XV *Ulysses S. Grant*, a month later, completing the initial order for five.

Presidential signed an agreement with Continental Airlines, announced on 12 January 1987, whereby it was to fly feeder services from 12 east coast cities into Dulles International for Continental, under the Continental Express banner; the 10 other airlines flying under this

name were operating mainly turboprops. In March that year 10 more 85-passenger 146 Series 200s were ordered to develop the new routes to be operated for Continental Express.

Among the new destinations to be served were Akron/Canton and Columbus in Ohio, Indianapolis (Indiana), Birmingham (Alabama), Savannah (Georgia) and Daytona Beach and Melbourne in Florida. The 146 was seen as filling a market gap between the 19-30 seater turboprop commuter airliners like the Jetstream 31 and Shorts 360, and larger types such as the Boeing 737 with 130 seats or more. In announcing the new 146 order Harold Pareti said: 'The fuel burn has been better than we could have expected and the low environmental noise level of the BAe146 is becoming a legend'. The 737s were to be phased out by the end of 1987, but meanwhile 10 more 737-200s were leased from Aviation Sales, the first four in May 1987, to provide capacity until the 10 146s in the repeat order were all delivered; this order included the earlier option on seven 146 Series 200s. In the end only thee of this repeat order were delivered, the first, N406XV, *Franklin D. Roosevelt*, leaving Hatfield on delivery on 18 March 1987, followed by the second, N407XV, on 26 June and the third, N408XV *Harry S. Truman*, on 4 August. N407XV was registered to BAe as G-BNKJ on 26 May for static display at the 1987 Paris Salon Internationale de l'Aéronautique, and became G-5-069 briefly just before delivery.

In February 1989, N408XV was leased by British Airways through BAe to make up capacity on its Scottish routes pending the late delivery of its BAe ATP turboprops on order. After a proving flight from Glasgow to Inverness, Stornoway and Benbecula on 22 February, N408XV flew its first British Airways service from Glasgow to Belfast on the 26th; it flew its last BA service on 31 August and a month later was registered G-BRNG to BAe. N407XV was also leased to BA through BAe, and flew its first BA service, from Glasgow to Benbecula, on 27 March, and its last service, from Belfast to Manchester, on 23 June; it was restored to BAe as G-BNKJ on 25 August.

Meanwhile, Presidential had ceased operating as a Continental Express carrier on 6 February 1988 and had transferred its allegiance to United Airlines, signing a five-year agreement to operate feeder services into United's Washington Dulles International hub under the United Express banner. Presidential was to handle connecting passengers between United flights into Dulles and the smaller cities in the northeastern USA which it now served.

According to Harold J. Pareti, the new alliance with United would enable his airline to remain independent, while assuming a major feeder role at Dulles, eventually replacing Air Wisconsin, which would then concentrate on a similar role at Chicago's O'Hare Airport. The reason for Presidential's changeover to United from Continental was that the latter had been cutting back its flights into Dulles, while United had been increasing its operations into the Dulles hub to 87 flights a day; at the time of the changeover, Presidential was operating 50 flights a day from Dulles.

But the hope of eventually displacing Air Wisconsin from the Dulles hub was to be unfounded, for — sadly— Presidential filed for Chapter 11 bankruptcy in October 1989, listing $30 million in assets and $74.4 million in liabilities. Services to seven of the 24 markets it served were suspended, and nearly 200 of its

774 employees were laid off (including about half the 210 pilots), while Presidential struggled to keep operating while working out reorganisation and refinancing plans under its Chapter 11 bankruptcy; the airline continued operating about 65% of its pre-bankruptcy schedules, carrying between 1,100 and 1,200 passengers daily. With eight 146s, seven BAe Jetstream 31s and two Beech 190s, Presidential had been one of BAe's best customers in the States in recent years, but BAe was now one of its major creditors. Of the 146s, N406XV was due to go to Discovery Airways of Honolulu, Hawaii, a newly-formed airline that had just ordered five 146 Series 200s and seven 146 Series 300s, plus two on option to operate inter-island services; all the 146s are to be leased. This order is worth $300 million, and scheduled services were due to start in December 1989, with plans to develop an extensive system of inter-island routes. This was not the first expression of interest in the 146 from these islands, for late in 1985 Hawaiian Airlines Inc, the major inter-island airline, had signed a memorandum of understanding with BAe to purchase eight 146 Series 200s, plus two more on option, for delivery beginning in November 1986. However, early in 1986 Hawaiian cancelled its plans to buy 146s and purchased additional DC-9s instead.

More UK Orders
Another island group which chose the 146 for its inter-island services was the Azores, where the local airline SATA (Servico Açoreano de Transportes Aéreos), also sometimes known as Air Azores, ordered a single 146 Series 200 in 1987 and, pending its delivery, leased 146 Series

100 G-BRJS from BAe, which had previously served with the RAF's No 10 Squadron as ZD695 and had completed the second of two spells on lease to Dan-Air Services on 7 June 1987. This left Hatfield on delivery to SATA at its Ponta Delgada base on 27 July and returned to Hatfield at the end of its lease on 30 September; it was shortly after re-registered G-OJET for lease to Manx Airlines. It was originally envisaged that the 146 Series 200 would be used to open services between the Azores and Portugal itself, but in the end SATA elected to confine itself to the inter-island services it had always flown, and three BAe ATP turboprops were ordered in place of the 146 to supplement the airline's three BAe748s. These linked all but one of the nine islands in the Azores archipelago, namely Santa Maria, Sao Miguel, (where SATA's base of Ponta Delgada is located), Terceira, Graciosa, Sao Jorge, Pico, Faial and Flores.

Although Dan-Air had been, in September 1982, the first British independent to place a firm order for the 146 and had been the first airline to put the type into scheduled service, it was to be another five years before a second British independent order for the 146 was placed. This was from Manx Airlines, one of the Airlines of Britain Group since 1988, when British Midland Airways took over complete control, for one 146 Series 100, and G-OJET, fresh from its recent lease to SATA in the Azores as G-BRJS, was delivered from Hatfield on lease from BAe on 30 November 1987, replacing a One-Eleven leased previously. Fitted out to seat 85 passengers, G-OJET flew its first service on 4 December from Ronaldsway to London Heathrow, this route being flown thrice-daily. Load factors averaging 70% were being experienced early in 1988 because a strike had affected regular sailings from the Isle of Man to the mainland, and this same strike called for additional air freight services to keep the island supplied with perishable food, these being provided by TNT 146-QT Quiet Trader operated by Air Foyle.

An unusual promotional gift made to mark the 146's introduction by Manx Airlines was a £2 Manx coin featuring the Queen's head on one side and the BAe146 on the other, the first time that an aircraft has been featured on UK coinage. This coin was made available in the Isle of Man in a presentation case, and was also sold in flight to passengers on the Manx 146. Manx Airlines was formed in 1982 by British Midland Airways and Air UK (the latter being part of the British and Commonwealth Shipping Co Group), and started operations from Ronaldsway on 1 November that year. The 146 is used exclusively on the Ronaldsway-Heathrow route, while of Manx's other aircraft, a SAAB SF340A flies the Liverpool-Heathrow services, four Shorts 360s fly services from Ronaldsway to Manchester, Blackpool, Glasgow, Belfast (City Airport) and Dublin, with a Viscount 836 serving as a back-up aircraft on the routes to Liverpool, Blackpool and Belfast. Manx was the only airline to operate both the 146 and the Viscount at the same time, these two types representing a generation gap of 30 years in British airliner design.

Air UK Ltd, the co-founder of Manx Airlines and now Britain's third largest scheduled airline, itself ordered two 98-passenger 146 Series 200s late in 1987 and a third on 30 December that year. The first, G-CNMF, was delivered from Hatfield on 27 November and flew its first service, from Guernsey to London Heathrow, on 14 December; it operated a routine of six sectors a day linking Guernsey and the Channel Islands with Southampton and Heathrow. The second and third 146s, G-CHSR and G-CSJH, left on delivery on 30 March and 7 April 1988

Below:
Manx Airlines acquired 146 Series 100, G-OJET (once ZD695 of No 10 Squadron) for services between Ronaldsway and London-Heathrow, linking the Isle of Man to London. G-OJET flew its first service on this route on 4 December 1987. *Olivier Constant*

respectively, and were based in Scotland, one serving the Aberdeen-Edinburgh-Amsterdam route and the other flying between Glasgow, Newcastle and Amsterdam. The latter route was formerly flown by KLM Royal Dutch Airlines which, in 1987, had acquired a 14.9% holding in Air UK, the remaining 85.1% of shares until recently being owned by the Bricom Group (British and Commonwealth Shipping). In 1988, Air UK transferred its headquarters to Stansted, London's third airport, and now operates an extensive domestic network from Scotland and Northern Ireland down to the Channel Islands. It also serves Amsterdam from nine UK airports, and flies services to Bergen and Stavanger in Norway as well as to Paris, Brussels and Zurich.

Air UK was formed on 1 January 1980 by the merger of four other airlines, British Island Airways, BIA/Air West, Air Anglia and Air Wales, all of which were members of the British and Commonwealth Shipping Group. The present fleet, in addition to the 146s, consists of 18 Fokker F27 Friendships and two Short 360s. Air UK also used 146 Series 200, G-BNND (ex-N192US of Pacific Southwest), on lease from 15 December 1988 to 12 March 1989, and 146 Series 100, C-GNVX, of the Canadian operator Air Nova (previously Royal West's N802RW) was, after a spell on lease to Air BC of Vancouver, returned to the UK. Here it was registered G-UKPC for lease to Air UK on 4 April 1989, flying its first Air UK service on 15 May. Two 146 Series 300s were ordered for the former British Caledonian routes from London Gatwick to Edinburgh and Glasgow taken over by Air UK in October 1988, and a further four Series 300s were ordered later in 1989. More 146 services from Stansted were introduced in the autumn of that year, beginning with routes to Amsterdam and Jersey.

A second ex-Air Nova 146 Series 100, G-UKJF (ex-C-GNVY), was delivered on 9 January 1990, followed by a fourth Series 300, G-UKID, in March, and in July Air UK announced

plans to lease seven more 146s, to be made up of three new Series 300s, three secondhand Series 200s and a previously-owned Series 100. This has now been cut back to four: two new 300s and two secondhand 200s. These are to be acquired on five-year operating leases with a break clause at three years, and will make Air UK the largest 146 operator in Europe, with a fleet of 13.

The Scottish airline Loganair, based at Glasgow and, like Manx Airlines, one of the Airlines of Britain Group, ordered three 146 Series 200s in the summer of 1988. The first of these, G-OLCA, was delivered on 19 July that year and flew its first service, from Manchester to Edinburgh, on 1 August, with another flight from Manchester to Belfast (City Airport) that day, there being a morning and evening flight to Edinburgh from Manchester. The second 146, G-OLCB, was, with the prototype 146 Series 200 G-BMYE, demonstrated at London City Airport on 24 July to show that the exceptionally quiet 146 would be suitable for operating into the Docklands airport, which up to then had been licensed to take only the DHC Dash 7s of Brymon Airways and London City Airways (the latter is another carrier in the Airlines of Britain Group). The airport's dockland runway, only six miles

Above:
One of Air UK's three 146 Series 200s, G-CHSR, seen at London-Gatwick with a Tu-154 of the Hungarian airline Malev and a KLM DC-9 Series 32. *Jerry Hepworth*

Right:
Air UK is one of the very few airlines to operate the Series 100, 200 and 300 versions of the 146; seen here is Series 100, G-UKPC, formerly C-GNVX of Air Nova. *Fleet PR*

Above:
The Scottish airline Loganair, based at Glasgow, is one of the Airlines of Britain group and operates two 146 Series 200s. *Olivier Constant*

from the City of London, is a mere 1,030m long and only 762m of this can normally be used; there are also severe noise limitations based on the certification noise levels of the Dash-7. Special planning approval had to be obtained to allow the two 146s to fly into the airport, and the strong case for allowing 146 operations into London City had to be backed up by actual noise levels recorded in a real demonstration. So 24 noise monitors in all were installed by experts from the various local authorities, from BAe, from London City Airport and the Civil Aviation Authority.

The first 146 landing at the airport was made by Loganair's G-OLCB, flown by BAe Civil Division chief test pilot Peter Sedgwick, and this was followed by the prototype Series 200, G-BMYE, flown by Dan Gurney. The latter carried out a series of take-offs, overflights at 500ft and 2,000ft, and landings, which were repeated by one of the resident Dash 7s to provide a comparison of noise levels. Conditions for noise measurement were not ideal as there was a gusting crosswind, but the 146 was shown to be quieter than the Dash 7 on landing and taxiing Only immediately after lift-off was the 146 any noisier, but the balance was quickly restored after the two aircraft had become established in their climbs. Approaches down a 6° glideslope for use in visual or instrument conditions had been approved before the 146 demonstration flights, and such an approach gradient will be necessary to clear certain proposed buildings near the airport, while similar take-off considerations mean that the 146 is the only jet airliner that can realistically operate from London City. Because of the limited length of runway the 146 demonstrations were carried out at reduced weights, but these had very little effect on the noise footprint. A 169m runway extension will be necessary before the 146 can carry a representative payload out of it, but then the airport's capacity will be transformed from the 44 passengers over 400 miles of the Dash 7 to 90 passengers over 900 miles with the 146, a range sufficient to reach most of the European capitals. Local residents in their thousands turned out to watch the 146 demonstrations, and showed great enthusiasm, with only a few complaints.

After the London City demonstrations, delivery of G-OLCB to Loganair was deferred; instead it went to American Airlines on lease from BAe for use over the former AirCal routes, for which American had previously leased the former Royal West N801RW as N720BA. G-OLCB left Hatfield on delivery to American on 22 October 1988, retaining its UK registration, and flew its first service for American from San Francisco to Los Angeles on 31 October and its last service, from Orange Country to San Jose, on 1 April 1989; it was then returned to BAe and delivered to Loganair on 31 May.

Loganair's first 146, G-OLCA, was wet-leased to British Airways for three months in 1990, flying its first service for BA between Manchester and Glasgow on 1 May; it also flew services between Manchester and Hanover. After the BA lease ended on 31 July it was wet-leased again for three months to the newly-formed Spanish charter operator Nordjet, being delivered to them on 1 August. For this lease the 146 was based at Palma, Majorca, and flew services from Palma to London Gatwick and to Teesside, as well as other routes serving San Sebastian, Madrid, Barcelona, Alicante, Malaga and Salamanca, as well as Vittoria, capital of the Basque region.

Loganair's third 146 had been ordered to operate the former British Caledonian routes from London Gatwick to Edinburgh and Glasgow for which Loganair, as well as Air UK, had applied to operate, but when Air UK was awarded them the order for the third 146 lapsed. By 1990-91, Mr Michael Bishop, chairman of the Airlines of

Britain Group, expects 8-10 146s to be operated by his Group. London City Airways is certain to order 146s, as the Docklands airport's owner, John Mowlem & Co, has now applied for planning consent for a 169m runway extension, amended noise limits to allow new types such as the 146, Dash 8, ATR 42 and Fokker 50 to operate into London City, and increases in operating hours and aircraft movements permitted.

The latest US regional to operate the 146 is WestAir Commuter, also known as United Express Airline, of Fresno, California, which ordered six 146 Series 200s plus three on option in November 1987. The first of these, N290UE, left Hatfield on delivery on 16 December 1987 and was followed by N291UE on 19 December and N292UE on the 22nd of that month. WestAir had signed a marketing agreement with United in June 1986 to provide feeder services for the latter at its San Francisco and Los Angeles hubs under the United Express banner, and about this time also became known as United Express Airline; it now served over two dozen destinations in California.

Its 90-passenger 146s began serving cities like Fresno, Redding and Eureka at the northern end of the Californian corridor, which could not have been served profitably by United's larger aircraft, and linking them to San Francisco, and later the BAe jets started non-stop flights between San Francisco and Palm Springs. Of the next three 146s, N293UE left on delivery on 15 April 1988, N294UE on 5 August and N295UE on 27 July; WestAir also leased the former Air Pac 146 Series 100, N146AP, from BAe from

22 April to 12 May 1988. To speed the introduction of the 146 into WestAir service Presidential Airways, which operated 146s into Washington Dulles, provided the airline with an initial training and support service package. Formed in 1972 as STOL Air, the airline was acquired in 1978 by an investment group and merged with Golden Eagle Airlines, thus becoming WestAir Airlines. In January 1983, after a management buy-out, WestAir Holdings Inc was formed, and in July 1987 established NPA as a subsidiary operating in the Pacific northwest. In December 1989 Atlantic Coast Airlines was formed in Washington, DC. The combined WestAir Holdings fleet number the six 146s, also 30 EMB-120 Brasilias (with ten more on order), two Short 360s and 57 Jetstream 31s.

The 146 was as much at home serving remote island communities as in the high-density traffic environment of California; an example of the former was the Faroe Islands some 200 miles north of the Shetlands and, like the latter, predominantly a fishing community. The Faroes belong to Denmark but have been self-governing since 1947, and in 1988 a new airline, Atlantic Airways, owned jointly by the Faroes Government and the Danish airline Cimber Air, started operations with a 146 Series 200. This was the former N193US and N369PS of Pacific Southwest/USAir which, as OY-CRG, flew the first Atlantic Airways service from Vagar Airport, Soervagur in the Faroes to Copehagen's Kastrup Airport on 28 March 1988, having been delivered from Southend five days before. It is registered to Cimber Air and operated by them for Atlantic Airways. The first air service to the Faroes had been started in 1963 when Icelandair made the islands a stopping place on its Reykjavik-Oslo route operated by Viscount 759s, and later the Danish carrier Danair A/S flew from Copenhagen to the Faroes via Bergen in Norway. OY-CRG overran the runway at Vagar on landing on 2 August 1989, but was soon repaired and back in service.

Perhaps the most remote and exotic of all the countries served by 146 is the Himalayan mountain kingdom of Bhutan, on India's northeast frontier between Assam and Tibet, and adjacent to Sikkim. One 146 Series 100 was ordered by Druk-Air Corporation (Royal Bhutan Airlines) at the end of 1987, this national airline taking its name from Druk Yul, meaning 'Kingdom of the Thundering Dragon', which is the local name for Bhutan. Registered A5-RGD (and previously G-BOEA of British Aerospace), Druk-Air's 146 left Hatfield on delivery on 18 November 1988 and flew its first service on the 25th from Paro, one of the chief towns of Bhutan, to Delhi. Druk-Air was formed on 1 April 1981 and began operations on 11 February 1983 when a Dornier

Above:
The Faroe Islands, some 200 miles north of the Shetlands, are served by Atlantic Airways with 85-seat ex-PSA 146 Series 200, OY-CRG, which flew the airline's first service, from Vagar Airport, Soervagur, in the Faroes to Copenhagen's Kastrup Airport on 28 March 1988.

Right:
Serving the Himalayan mountain kingdom of Bhutan, between Asam and Tibet, is Druk-Air (Royal Bhutan Airlines), which flies 146 Series 100, A5-RGD, on services from Paro, airport of the capital city of Thimphu, at an elevation of 6,950ft, to Calcutta and Dhaka in India and also to Bangkok. The 146 is also leased to Indian Airlines Corporation for 1,000hr a year.

Do228-200 flew its first scheduled service from Paro to Calcutta; this inaugural flight, which took just under 11/2hrs to cover the 375 miles, took off to the incantations of a Tibetan monk.

Before Druk-Air started operations, Bhutan's only link with India was a poor-quality road, and the journey by car took 16hr from the nearest Indian airport, at Badogra, at the foot of the Himalayas in western Bengal. The airfield at Paro, the only one in the country, has an elevation of 6,950ft and is accessible only through narrow valleys. It was built for the Bhutanese Government by the Indian Border Road Organisation, and Druk-Air itself had been set up with the assistance of senior personnel from Indian Airlines Corporation — IAC; the 146 is leased by IAC for 1,000hr a year for use over its northern domestic routes, and the two Do228s (a second was delivered in September 1983) have been leased at various times to the Indian regional airline Vayudoot, a subsidiary of IAC. Druk-Air's present routes link Paro to Calcutta and Dhaka, and charter flights are also undertaken. Bhutan's external affairs are guided by the Indian Government, and the country has valuable forests, exporting timber and cardamom (a variety of spice).

Top:
Air BC of Vancouver, British Columbia, was the first Canadian 146 customer, currently operating five Series 200s over routes serving British Columbia, the Yukon, Alberta and also Seattle in the USA.

Above:
Air Nova flies four 146 Series 200s over a network serving the Canadian maritime provinces, especially Nova Scotia, New Brunswick, Newfoundland and Labrador. It started operations with a pair of ex-Royal West 146 Series 100s leased from BAe.

Canadian Operations

First Canadian customer for the 146 was Air BC Ltd of Vancouver, British Columbia, which ordered three 146 Series 200s plus three on option in the spring of 1988; two of these options were converted into firm orders in December that year. Air BC had considered the One-Eleven, the Fokker F28 Fellowship and a stretched version of the Canadair Challenger executive jet, but chose the 146 for several reasons, including its ability to operate from a 5,000ft runway and to land on gravel strips, while its quietness would be an advantage in serving cities like Edmonton, Alberta. Air BC serves 30 destinations in British Columbia, five in neighbouring Alberta, Whitehorse and Yellowknife in the Yukon and also Seattle; at many of these places it faces strong competition from another Canadian regional, Time Air.

Air BC was formed on 1 November 1980 by the amalgamation of five small airlines serving the Pacific coastal and Vancouver Island regions of British Columbia; this resulted in a combined fleet of about 100 aircraft, many of them float planes, ranging from the Cessna 172 to the DC-3 in size. A process of cutbacks and rationalisation was put in hand, and by 1984 the fleet consisted of three Dash 7s and 14 Twin Otters. That year flights to the interior of British Columbia began, in the face of fierce competition on fares, and from October 1983 to 1986 Air BC operated feeder services for CP Air into the Vancouver hub under the name Canadian Pacific Commuter. In April 1987 the airline was acquired by Air Canada, for whom it now operates feeder services under the name Air Canada Conector.

The 146s seat 85 passengers and the first, C-FBAB, was delivered on 13-14 May 1988, flying Air BC's first 146 service (a charter flight) from Vancouver to Prince Rupert on 20 May. The second, C-FBAE, was delivered on 7-9 June and was followed by C-FBAF a few days later. Before the 146s arrived, Air BC was scheduling 916 flights a week with its Dash 7s and Twin Otters, and the 146s were put on to the longer, thinner routes mostly serving places at least 400 miles apart; the first 146 started services from Vancouver to Prince Rupert and Terrace/Kitimat, while the second and third aircraft enabled jet services to be extended to Prince George and Fort St John, to Kelowna in southern British Columbia and to Whitehorse in the Yukon. Two more 146s were delivered, C-FBAO leaving Hatfield for Vancouver on 24 January 1989, followed by C-FBAV a month later, and Series 100, C-GNVX (formerly Royal West's N802RW), was leased by Air BC from 20 January for two months, after a spell on lease to Air Nova. The airline also has two Dash 8-100s and six Dash 8-300s on order to supplement the six Dash 8-100s it already has, and six BAe Jetstream 31s were scheduled for delivery in 1989.

The second Canadian customer for the 146 was Air Nova Inc of Halifax, Nova Scotia, which ordered two 85-passenger 146 Series 200s in August 1988, plus two more on option. Pending delivery of the first two, a pair of ex-Royal West Series 100s leased from BAe Inc and prepared for Air Nova service by AAR Inc at Oklahoma City, flew the first services, these seating 69 passengers in a five-abreast layout. The first of these, C-GNVX (formerly N802RW), was leased from 25 August 1988 and served until the following January, leaving Halifax on the 19th of that month for Vancouver for a further spell on

lease to Air BC. The second, C-GNVY (ex-N803RW), was leased from 2 September and was retained by Air Nova for just over a year, being returned to BAe on 1 October 1989 for conversion to a freighter.

First of the Series 200s was C-GRNZ, which left on delivery on 11 January 1989; this was the first 146 to be assembled at the new Woodford production line near Manchester and had first flown on 16 May 1988 as G-5-106. The second Air Nova Series 200, C-GRNY, was also Woodford-assembled and first flew as G-11-115, being the first Woodford 146 to make use of the Class B G-11- test registration; this left on delivery on 24 January 1989. The Woodford line was set up to increase 146 production from 28 to 40 a year by 1990; four aircraft were built here in 1988, building up progressively thereafter to a total of 100 over six years.

Air Nova began jet services on 5 September 1988 with a leased 146 serving Montreal and Ottawa from Fredericton and St John in New Brunswick, there being direct services from Moncton (New Brunswick) to Montreal; the 146s were soon serving Halifax as well as Gander and St John's in Newfoundland. Like Air BC, Air Nova is an Air Canada Connector airline, providing feeder services for Air Canada at Halifax. It was formed in May 1986 as a joint venture between the latter (which has a 49% holding), Halifax-based business interests and commuter airline Labrador Airways. Operations started in July that year with the first of seven Dash 8-100s, and Air Nova currently serves 18 destinations, mostly in Nova Scotia, New Brunswick, Newfoundland and Labrador, but also including Quebec, Boston (Mass), Montreal and Ottawa. Two more 146 Series 200s were ordered in February 1989, and the first, C-GRNX, left Hatfield on delivery on 13 July. This was followed by Air Wisconsin's N604AW, which was leased as C-FEXN from 11 June and returned to BAe in August, being re-registered G-OSUN. This was replaced by Series 200 C-GRNV (formerly G-BPUV) which, after reverting briefly to its test registration G-5-133, left Hatfield on delivery as C-RRNV on 29 September.

Thai Airways International, which had ordered two 146 Series 300s for domestic and regional routes at the end of 1988, with two more later, leased Series 200, G-BNND (the former N192US and N368PS of Pacific Southwest), as HS-TBQ from 1 April 1989; this left East Midlands on that day for delivery to Bangkok, having just finished an earlier spell on lease to Air UK, and flew its first Thai Airways service on 6 April, the first Series 300 being delivered later that month. HS-TBQ returned to BAe from lease in mid-September as G-BNND and was then due to go to the newly-formed Hawaiian carrier Discovery Airways, which was also due to take Presidential's former N406XV (returned to BAe in mid-September and now G-5-062). Discovery has three more Series 200s and seven Series 300s on order, plus two on option. To replace HS-TBQ, Thai Airways' International also acquired Series 100 HS-TBO for use on shorter, less-developed airfields previously limited to turboprops. Latest African customer for the Series 100 at the time of writing was Air Botswana, which ordered a single example in June 1989 for its domestic and regional routes; this, registered A2-ABD, was delivered in October 1989 and seats 77 passengers in a two-class interior. It entered service on routes from Gaborone (the capital) to Harare in Zimbabwe and Nairobi. A second 146 entered Air Botswana service on 29 January 1991 on routes from Gaboroney to Windhoek (Namibia), Dar-es-Salaam (Tanzania), Lilongwe (Malawi) and Lusaka (Zambia).

Latest UK operator of the 146 was Yorkshire-based regional Capital Airlines, which flew services from Leeds/Bradford Airport to London Gatwick, Jersey, Bristol, Cardiff, Dublin, Belfast and Glasgow, with a service to Brussels, started in the spring of 1989, as the latest addition to the network. Services from Luton to Belfast City Airport and from Luton to Dublin were also operated. Two of Air Wisconsin's 146 Series 200s that were traded in to BAe were

leased, N603AW becoming G-OSKI and being delivered to Capital on 16 August 1989, flying its first service on the 19th. The second, N604AW, after a spell on lease to Air Nova as C-FEXN, was registered to BAe as G-OSUN in August for service with Capital. One of the 146s was based at Leeds/Bradford and flew the Belfast route, and the other at Luton, where it replaced a leased Viscount on the Dublin route, also serving Belfast; both were fitted out to seat 106 passengers. Capital had been formed in 1983 as Brown Air Services, taking its present title in 1987, and it also operated six Short 360-300s.

Sadly, Capital Airlines went into liquidation on 27 June 1990 and a receiver was appointed; the two 146 Series 200s were grounded, along with the six Shorts 360-300s.

Of the former Presidential 146 Series 200s two — N401XV and N403XV — went to Chile's state airline LAN-Chile (Linea Aerea Nacional de Chile) at the beginning of 1990, the first as CC-CEJ, for use on domestic routes. The first for LAN-Chile flew its first service on 10 February 1990 still wearing its Presidential registration N401XV; it became CC-CEJ and its sister-ship N403XV was delivered to Santiago on 27 February, becoming CC-CET. LAN-Chile has now ordered a third Series 200 for delivery in the third quarter of 1990 to replace a 737-200, and one of its first two 146s became the world's first commercial jetliner to operate into Antarctica when it flew a route-proving service from Punta

Right:
The 146 Series 100 is still in demand for the smaller national airlines like Druk-Air and Air Botswana; the latter's A2-ABD, seen here, was delivered in October 1989 and links Gaborone, the capital, to Harare in Zimbabwe and Nairobi in Kenya.

Arenas in southern Chile to a Chilean Air Force base on King George Island, which had just an unprepared gravel runway used only by military C-130 Hercules transports. At least 19 passengers of the 65 aboard were killed when LAN-Chile 146 CC-CET overran the runway at Puerto Williams on Navarino Island on 20 February 1991. The 146 was en route to Antarctica from Punta Arenas on a charter flight for a US tour operator. N406XV went to Discovery Airways of Hawaii as N88ODV; Discovery is also taking delivery of Series 200s N881DV (ex-HS-TBQ), N882DV, N883DV and N884DV. At the end of 1989, BAe was seeking repossession of 10 out of Presidential's 12 aircraft following the airline's Chapter 11 bankruptcy. Sabena, Belgium's national airline, has ordered four Series 200s with four more on option for its Antwerp-based regional subsidiary Delta Air Transport NV, which flies services for Sabena and KLM in Europe; the 146s are taking over some of Sabena's more thinly-trafficked routes, such as those to Stockholm and Frankfurt. The first 146, OO-DJC (ex-N407XV of Presidential), was delivered on 1 December 1989 and flew its first service two days later, being followed soon after by OO-DJD, with OO-DJE and OO-DJF to join the fleet in June and July 1990. Delta's 146s are to open a new route from Antwerp to London City Airport. A repeat order by Sabena for four Series 200s plus four on option for Delta Air Transport was among the new orders for 25 announced just before Farnborough 1990.

The Swedish leasing company Salenia Aviation, which took over 146-QT operator Malmo Aviation in May 1989, is to have two Series 200s in 1991. In South Africa a 146 Series 200 was to have been acquired in October 1990 by Acorn Air, a subsidiary of the Air Crew Operating and Recruitment Network (Acorn) which is the business arm of SAAPA — the South African Airways Pilots' Association. This Series 200, with crew, will be leased out to other operators in southern Africa, and Acorn Air took delivery of a 146-200QC in April 1991.

Latest orders for the 146 Series 200 are for three from Air Atlantic of St John's, Newfoundland, for delivery in March and April 1990, and four plus eight on option from the Swiss regional airline Crossair, based at Basle. Air Atlantic currently operates 12 Dash 8-100s on routes linking Newfoundland to eastern Canada, to the French islands of St Pierre et Miquelon and to Boston (Maine), serving a total of 23 places. The airline operates as a 'Canadian Partner' providing feeder traffic to Canadian Airlines International at Montreal, Halifax and St John's. Crossair chose the 146 to meet heavy expected traffic demands and preferred it to the Fokker 100, not least because of its ability to operate from Lugano, where noise is a major consideration; the 146s are to be introduced on services from Zürich, Geneva and Venice to Lugano. Crossair had previously been restricted by Swiss law from operating jets, but an agreement was reached with Swissair, which owns 38% of the airline. Crossair has also acquired three 146 Series 200s from USAir, the first of which entered service in June 1990, serving as interim equipment pending delivery of Crossair's first 146s in October 1992, when Category III bad-weather landing equipment will be available for the type. Crossair currently serves 35 European cities, flying a number of routes for Swissair, and uses Saab 340As and 340Bs, of which it has 30 on order, as well as 25 of the stretched version of the 340, the Saab 2000.

Crossair began jet services with the first two of

its ex-USAir 146 Series 200s, HB-IXB (ex-N175US) and HB-IXC (ex-N190US) in June, the first of these, nicknamed *Jumbolino* by the airline, beginning Basle-Munich and Amsterdam flights on 18 June, and three weeks later starting services from Lugano to Zürich, Geneva and Venice. Seating 82 passengers, this 146 has modified brakes to permit quicker cooling and hence shorter turnround times at Lugano, Berne and Florence. The second 146, HB-IXC, arrived on 17 June for refurbishing to Crossair requirements, and the third is due for delivery in October. The airline plans to fly 146 services from Switzerland into London City Airport by the end of 1991.

Latest order for the Series 100 is one for the Indonesian operator PT National Air Charter for use on charters from Jakarta and Singapore; this was handed over to its new owners at Woodford on 6 April 1990, later becoming PK-DTA. This was followed by a second Series 100 G-BRLN, which became PK-DTC (this was one of the 25

new aircraft on order revealed just before Farnborough 1990), and also displayed in the static park at Farnborough was NAC's Series 200 G-BSOH, which became PK-DTD.

The first 146 order from Central America, from the Mexcian airline AVIACSA — Aviacion de Chiapas SA for two Series 200s, was announced in August, with deliveries scheduled for the latter month and December 1990. These will be AVIACSA's first jets, and will be operated with five-abreast seating for 90 passengers. AVIACSA is based at Tuxtla Gutierrez, the capital of Chiapas province bordering Guatemala, and its 146s will serve Mexico City, Tapachula, Minatitlan and Oaxaca. The 146 was chosen not least because its short field performance in 'hot and high' conditions enables it to serve remoter communites with short runways. The two 146s operate from the Tuxtla Gutierrez downtown airport named Francisco Sarabia. With this order an extensive demonstration and sales tour of Latin America was commenced using LAN-

Above:
Sabena of Belgium ordered four 146 Series 200s with four more on option for its Antwerp-based regional subsidiary Delta Air Transport NV, which flies various routes for Sabena and KLM in Europe. Delta's first, OO-DJC, seen here, flew its first service on 3 December 1989.

Right:
Still wearing its US registration N401XV, this ex-Presidential 146 Series 200 is seen at Arica Airport in central Chile in the livery of the state airline LAN-Chile. It was formally handed over at Washington on 8 January 1990 and became CC-CEJ.

Chile's third 146 Series 200 which, in addition to Mexico, will visit Bolivia, Ecuador, Argentina, Paraguay and Uruguay. AVIACSA's first 146 XA-RMO, formerly Presidential's N402XV, left on delivery on 20 September and flew its first service on the 23rd.

Alisarda, based on Olbia in Sardinia, became the second Italian operator after Sagittair to choose the 146 when it ordered four Series 200s with an option on four more, to be either 200s or 300s, in September 1990. The first four will be delivered in 1993 but pending delivery of these, four Series 200s are to be leased from BAe in April 1991. The airline would like to operate its 146s on services from Florence to London City Airport or, failing that, to Gatwick, at first once daily and then twice daily. Other routes that will be served by 146 are from Florence to Madrid, Barcelona, Paris, Frankfurt and Munich. Alisarda's new 146s to be delivered in 1993 will have the new Textron Lycoming LF507 turbofans and Category III autoland equipment. The airline

is to move its headquarters from Sardinia to Florence.

In March 1991, as part of a cost-cutting drive aimed at improving operating efficiency in the face of recessionary pressures and a weak dollar, British Aerospace announced job cutbacks from 35,600 to 30,900 in its Commercial Aircraft and Dynamics companies, together with the decision to transfer final assembly of BAe 146s from Hatfield to the Woodford plant. The number of employees at Hatfield would fall by 1,470 to 3,400, while 375 jobs were to go at Woodford, leaving 3,100 employees. Nose assemblies for the 146 would still be completed at Hatfield, and the Woodford plant, which had built 16 BAe 146s in 1990, would have to be more fully utilised since the TNT Group, to meet whose 146 demands the Woodford line had been set up, had itself been losing money and had not placed any further 146-QT orders for over two years. BAe has now cut almost 16,000 jobs in the past five years.

Military freighter versions of the BAe146 had been studied in 1973-74, and when the 146 programme was restarted in July 1978 it went ahead both in its basic civil form and as a military freighter version with a rear-loading ramp, as related in Chapter 3. First flight of the latter had originally been scheduled for August 1982 following government approval for the 146 programme's go-ahead, but development of a military variant was put back to enable top priority to be given to getting the 146 Series 100 and 200 flying and certificated. It was not until the 1987 Paris Salon Internationale de l'Aéronautique that firm details of the 146STA and other military variants were released, and it was not until a year later that the prototype 146STA made its first flight.

It had originally been intended that rear-loading military variants of the 146 were to be developed and marketed at Manchester, and the sale of no less than 100 of the original military version had been assumed in the financial planning behind the 146 programme's relaunch, even though the RAF at that time had no requirement for such a transport. But the market for military 146s was pre-empted not only by the larger Lockheed C-130 Hercules family, which were supplied to many Third World air forces, often as a part of foreign aid, and by Soviet types such as the Antonov An-12 and An-24 for countries in the Kremlin's sphere of influence, but also by much smaller designs such as the Spanish CASA C212 Aviocar and the CASA/IPTN CN-235 transport, a joint venture between Spain and Indonesia, which have also sold in some numbers to Third World (especially Latin American) air forces.

The original military version would have featured a loading ramp folding up into the rear fuselage, a strengthened freight floor and a loading strut under the rear fuselage just ahead of the ramp. Typical loads would have been a CVR(T) Scorpion tank weighing 17,500lb and a half-ton truck; a one-ton truck, a 105mm field gun and a half-ton truck, or up to 70 fully-equipped paratroops. Optional long range fuel tanks of a total capacity of 486imp gal could be fitted in the underfloor cargo holds. Powerplants were to have been four of the 7,500lb st Avco Lycoming F102 turbofans from which the ALF 502 was derived, the latter being a derated version of the F102, which had powered the Northrop A-9A, the losing entry in the USAF's AX close support aircraft competition which was won by the Fairchild A-10 Thunderbolt II. BAe Hatfield did have discussions with the RAF at this time about their future short range tactical transport requirements but, as one BAe official said, 'It is always difficult at this early stage to obtain the customer's clear views, especially when he is

The 146STA (for Sideloading Tactical Airlifter), of which the prototype G-BSTA is seen here, is in effect a military variant of the civil 146-QT, and has a cargo door of the same size in the port side. It can carry up to 60 paratroops, or 80 passengers or 18 stretcher cases, plus 26 sitting casualties in the 'cas evac' role, or six pallets for rapid airdrops.
M. J. Hardy

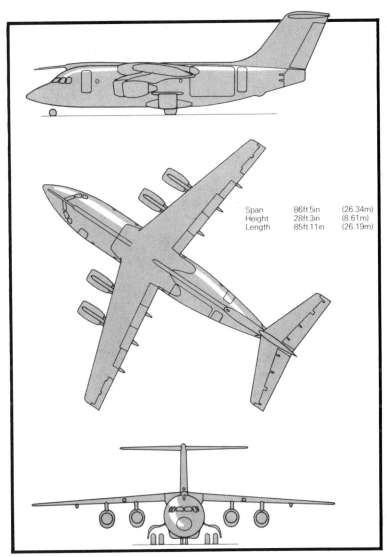

Span   86ft 5in   (26.34m)
Height   28ft 3in   (8.61m)
Length   85ft 11in   (26.19m)

General arrangement drawing of 146STA

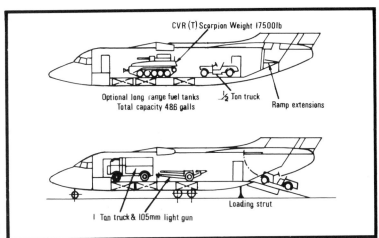

CVR (T) Scorpion Weight 17500lb

Optional long range fuel tanks
Total capacity 486 galls

½ Ton truck

Ramp extensions

1 Ton truck & 105mm light gun

Loading strut

This drawing shows the original military 146 that preceded the 146STA, which had a rear loading ramp and was originally scheduled to fly in August 1982.

preoccupied with sharp-end aeroplane budgets'. Also, military orders could not realistically be expected until the 146 had proved itself in airline use.

At the 1987 Paris Salon, BAe announced details of four new military variants of the 146: the BAe146STA (for Sideloading Tactical Airlifter), the 146MSL (Military Side Loader), the 146M (Military Tanker) and the 146M (Military Rear Loader). Of these only the 146STA is now current; the 146M (Military Rear Loader) would have featured a rear-loading ramp folding up behind hydraulically-operated rear doors similar to the original military freighter; the other variants having a large side-loading door which the original military version did not have. All these variants could have been fitted with a flight refuelling probe projecting from the flightdeck, and the 146STA tanker is fitted with two hose drum refuelling pods mounted under the wingtips, quick-change fuel tanks mounted on pallets in the cabin and a closed-circuit TV system with wingtip to wingtip field of view for the pilots. As a tanker the 146STA can provide a transferable load of 25,000lb of fuel at a radius of 230 miles.

The 146STA is derived from the civil 146-QT Quiet Trader freighter as used by the TNT group of operators, and can carry up to 22,300lb of military freight on the strengthened floor, which is stressed to take loads of up to 200lb/sq ft. The STA variant has the ability to operate from forward airfields and offers the military user low life cycle costs. It has a 10ft 11in wide x 6ft 4in high upward-opening cargo door (the same size as that of the 146-QT) in the port side of the rear fuselage, and this door allows maximum flexibility in loading military vehicles as well as field guns or more conventional palletised loads. An air openable sliding door is set behind the main cargo door and this, together with an outward-opening door opposite on the starboard side, opens outwards and forwards hydraulically to allow the dropping of paratroops, of whom up to 60 can be carried in full combat gear on inward-facing canvas seats. When open, these two doors act as airflow deflectors for paratroops making their jump. Up to 80 personnel can be carried in airline-type seats at 33in pitch in the staff transport role, and dividers can be installed in the cabin to turn part of it into a command area or VIP section.

The port side sliding door can be opened in flight to a maximum width of 5ft 0in, which allows standard 4ft 6in x 4ft 0in air-drop containers to be dropped on re-supply missions. Roller tracks can be fitted to the existing seat rails to facilitate the movement of pallets, and a self-contained loading ramp is carried. Six pallets can be carried on guide rails for rapid airdrops, and there are

five pallet positions stressed to take a load of 4,000lb and one to take 7,000lb; the maximum palletised payload that can be carried is 20,750lb.

In the 'casevac' role the 146STA can carry up to 18 stretcher cases plus 26 sitting wounded and four medical attendants. The STA can also be used in the search and rescue role, for which the weather radar is switched to surveillance mode, and typically 12 dinghies can be dropped through the sliding paratroop door. In this role the STA can loiter on station for 4.4hrs at a distance of 230 miles from base. The 146STA's cabin size, with an unobstructed length of 43ft 11in and a maximum width of 10ft 11in, offers obvious possibilities for crew trainer or AEW versions at some future date.

The prototype 146STA, registered G-BSTA on 12 July 1988, had started life as the second development 146, G-SSHH, which, after a sales tour of China and the Far East in 1984, had served with Royal West as N801RW and was later leased to Dan-Air as G-BPNP and to American Eagle as N720BA. It was earmarked for a further lease to Manx Airlines as G-BPNP but instead was flown out to Hayes International Corporation at Dothan, Alabama, for conversion to the prototype 146STA. Hayes had been contracted by BAe to do the freighter conversion of the 146 Series 200 into the 146-QT, and they were likewise contacted by BAe to complete the prototype STA conversion; this first flew in its 146STA form on 8 August 1988. At this time Hayes International Corp was in the process of being taken over by Pemco Aeroplex of Birmingham, Alabama, a subsidiary of Precision Standard Inc of Denver, Colorado, the takeover was completed in September and Hayes International became absorbed into Pemco Aeroplex. Because G-BPNP was a Series 100 while production STA conversions will be of Series 200 standard, the main cargo door was installed forward of the rear passenger door, and was slightly different in size, being 10ft 10in wide x 6ft 6in high, Pemco Aeroplex also obtained an FAA supplemental type certificate for the 146STA, and will do production STA conversions.

G-BSTA was displayed in the static park at the 1988 SBAC Show in green and sand camouflage, and later left Hatfield for a sales tour of Australasia and the Far East which lasted 36 days, in which the 146STA flew over 30,000 miles and 116hr without any snags. It was demonstrated to the Royal Australian Air Force (RAAF), and appeared at the RAAF Bicentennial Display at Richmond, near Sydney, on 12-16 October. A highlight of its demonstration to the RAAF was its operation into and out of an unpaved 1,300m airstrip at a place called

Above:
This view shows the 146STA's cargo door open and a ramp for loading tracked vehicles. *M. J. Hardy*

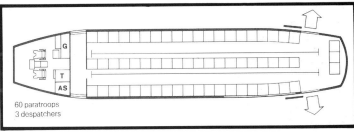

60 paratroops
3 despatchers

Dual exit paratrooping layout

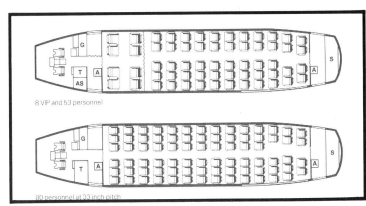

8 VIP and 53 personnel

80 personnel at 33 inch pitch

VIP/Personnel transport layouts

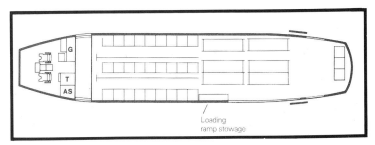

Loading
ramp stowage

Stretcher/Casevac layout

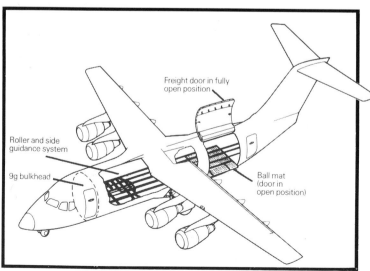

Freight door in fully open position

Roller and side guidance system

9g bulkhead

Ball mat (door in open position)

Freight handling drawing

Puk-Puk, the first time that a jet of the 146's size and payload capacity had flown into such a small forward airstrip. The 146STA later flew on to New Zealand where it was demonstrated to the Royal New Zealand Air Force in Wellington and Auckland. It then flew to Halim Air Base in Indonesia for a two-week tour of South-East Asia, where it was shown to a number of air forces, visiting Brunei, Singapore, Malaysia and the Thai capital of Bangkok. The 146STA, together with two BAe Hawks for which it was providing logistical support, gave a joining flying display at Bangkok International Airport which was closed for 20min while the BAe aircraft performed.

Production 146STAs will have ALF 502R-MR turbofans and a fuel capacity of 3,384 USgals (2,818 imp gal) — slightly different tankage to that of the 146 Series 200. An EFIS flightdeck would be standard, and one of this type has been undergoing flight development on BAe's 146 Series 300, G-OAJF, since 19 April 1989. Maximum payload of the 146STA is 22,750lb, and maximum take-off weight is 93,000lb. The 146M (Military Rear Loader) variant, which is no longer current, would have had large hydraulically-operated rear loading doors with a fold-up ramp, allied to a lower main deck floor which can take larger and heavier payloads than the 146STA. This variant would have a redesigned main landing gear in a tandem configuration and housed in under-fuselage sponsons.

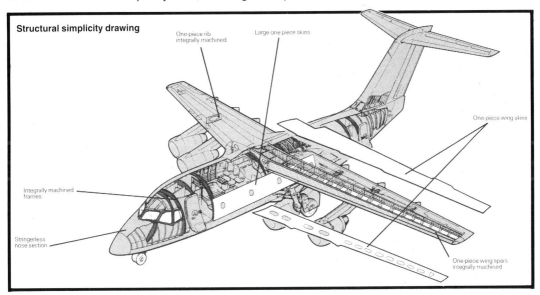

Structural simplicity drawing

One-piece rib integrally machined
Large one piece skins
One-piece wing skins
Integrally machined frames
Stringerless nose section
One-piece wing spars integrally machined

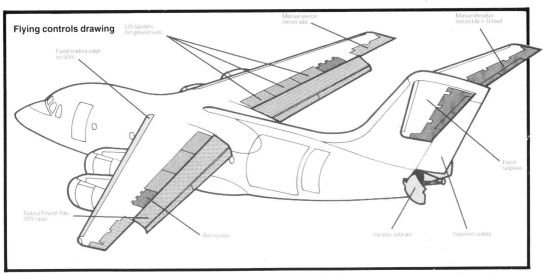

Flying controls drawing

Lift-spoilers (on ground use)
Fixed leading edge no slats
Manual aileron (servo tab)
Manual elevator (servo tab + Q-feel)
Fixed tailplane
Tabbed Fowler flap, 78% span
Roll spoiler
Variable airbrake
Powered rudder

The 146-QT Quiet Trader

First 146 to be used as a freighter was the Series 100, N146AP, of the Alaskan operator Air Pac Inc (Air Pacific Airlines) of Dutch Harbour in the Aleutians. As related in Chapter 4, this 146 seated either 76 passengers at 33/32in pitch or carried a mixed payload of 40 passengers in the rear of the cabin and four freight containers, which could each carry 1,500lb of cargo, in the forward part of the cabin. Air Pac carried a good deal of freight, including king crabs flown out of Dutch Harbour for dining tables on the Alaskan mainland, but it ceased operations in May 1986 and three of its former executives later filed lawsuits against BAe and Textron Lycoming.

First orders for the 146, from operators such as Dan-Air, Air Wisconsin and Pacific Southwest, had all been for passenger variants, but there were obvious possibilities in a freighter version of the 146 Series 200, which duly appeared as the 146-QT Quiet Trader. The name is a reminder that air freight is very often flown at night, and the 146's exceptional quietness, as demonstrated in stringent noise measurement tests at such noise-conscious airports as Osaka in Japan and Orange County's John Wayne Airport in California, made it eminently suitable for the development of night freight services.

Allied to this is a capacious cargo hold, the cargo floor being 52ft 9in long and 10ft 7in wide, and the ability to carry six standard 108in x 88in pallets, with space for an extra half-pallet measuring 53in x 88in, or up to nine standard LD3 containers. The floor is stressed for a maximum individual pallet load of 6,000lb in one stressed area for one pallet, and 4,000lb elsewhere, and minor modifications to the freight floor make possible a maximum payload of 24,300lb of cargo. Later, further structural developments enable payloads of up to 28,600lb to be carried. The hydraulically-operated upward-opening freight door is, like that of the 146STA, 10ft 11in wide and 6ft 4in high; for the freighter conversion of the Series 100, of which a few have been made, the main cargo door is 9ft 7in wide and 6ft 4in high. For both variants the floor sill height is 6ft 4in. The main cargo door hinges upwards through a total of 160° and can be held steady at any point in its travel, being locked in the closed position by eight claws; it is controlled from a panel next to the crew access door.

A 9g bulkhead is fitted which allows the flightcrew limited access to the cargo area during flight. A smoke detection system is installed for when hazardous cargoes are carried, together

Below:
A BAe146 undergoes painting in the hangar at Marshall of Cambridge (Engineering) Ltd. By September 1990 Marshall's had painted over 40 BAe146s which it receives in a 'green' condition from Hatfield, and has three or four in the hangar at any one time undergoing the application of airline liveries. *Marshall of Cambridge*

with a means of shutting off the ventilation system to the freight compartment, and any noxious gases produced by the cargo can be excluded from the flightdeck. The underfloor holds of the passenger 146 Series 200 are retained to provide cargo space for urgent loose-loaded packages that need to be quickly unloaded; these holds have a capacity of 645cu ft and can carry a load of 6,670lb. With an all-palletised load, which is how the TNT Group operates its 146s, a turn-round time of 20min can be achieved. The 146-QT can also be used in a mixed or Combi interior configuration, with passenger accommodation at the front of the cabin and freight at the rear, the rear passenger door being retained separately.

In the spring of 1986, BAe selected Hayes International Corporation of Dothan, Alabama, to undertake freighter conversions of the 146. It produced the first such conversion, of Series 200 N146FT, and was responsible for the design, manufacture and installation of the cargo door, freight handling equipment, internal structural reinforcements and furnishings.

Hayes International, which was taken over and absorbed by Pemco Aeroplex in September 1988, first became known in this country in the 1950s with the conversion of 112 Boeing B-50 Superfortresses into the KB-50J triple-hose tanker variant, with two J47-GE-23 turbojets in underwing nacelles to boost speed and climb. It later produced a number of freighter conversions of airliners, including the Convair 340, 440 and 580 and the Lockheed L-1011 TriStar.

The prototype 146-QT conversion, N146FT, first flew on 20 March 1986 with the test registration G-5-056, and left Hatfield for conversion at Hayes' Dothan facility a week later. In August it became N146QT and in December 1986 was sold to the TNT Group as G-TNTA, actually being registered to TNT Roadfreight (UK) Ltd, being handed over to TNT on 5 May 1987 and flying its first service the same day.

The TNT Group (the initials stand for Thomas Nationwide Transport) is an Australian transportation group that can now claim to be the largest diversified transport business in the world, currently operating in 105 countries. It operates a nationwide surface transport network across Australia, and in 1980 the TNT Group, together with Mr Rupert Murdoch's News International Corporation, became in effect joint owners of Ansett Transport Industries — ATI, the parent company of the Ansett group of airlines, when they acquired over 99% of ATI, which had previously had nearly 18,000 ordinary shareholders. TNT specialises in express deliveries and its subsidiary IPEC's 'Elite' service guarantees delivery of freight packages next day,

often before noon, throughout much of Western Europe.

It is TNT's policy to control all the links in the transport/distribution chain themselves and this led to air express operations being started from Birmingham Airport in November 1985 by TNT-IPEC Ltd for its 'Elite' service deliveries from the UK to West Germany. Four round trips a week were flown from Birmingham to Hannover and from Birmingham to Nuremburg using two Handley Page Heralds chartered through TNT-IPEC's broker, Air Foyle, from such operators as Air Bridge, Euroair and Channel Express. Birmingham's proximity to the M1 motorway enabled inbound cargoes from these flights to be rushed by lorry under Customs bond to TNT's UK hub at Northampton, and a Boeing 737-200QC was leased from Aer Lingus in October 1986 for flights from Birmingham to Dublin.

Having successfully tested and proved the viability of air express services from Birmingham using chartered aircraft, TNT was able to make the next step towards operating its own fleet. This was to carry out an intensive two-night evaluation of the prototype 146-QT, N146QT — made available by BAe — over TNT-IPEC's express service routes on the nights of 10 and 11 November 1986. Being ferried to Dublin on the 9th, N146QT flew the regular TNT-IPEC schedule from Dublin via Birmingham to Nuremburg and Hannover and returned via Birmingham to Dublin, on two consecutive nights. Loads carried were mainly in the lightweight parcels category, loaded on pallets and secured by netting, and one object of these proving trials was to ensure the 146-QT's compatibility with existing cargo-handling facilities at the airports on the route. Special emphasis was also placed on noise readings recorded at these airports, which confirmed that the 146 could be permitted to operate throughout night-time curfew hours, thus allowing its operators greater flexibility in scheduling their freight flights, while keeping noise nuisance to the minimum.

So successful were these trials that, as related earlier, TNT purchased the 146-QT, which became G-TNTA and was handed over in a ceremony at Birmingham Airport on 5 May 1987; TNT placed a firm order for two more 146-QTs with two on option. In announcing the acquisition of G-TNTA the previous December, TNT's Managing Director Sir Peter Abeles said that the BAe146's proven reputation as the world's quietest jetliner made it ideally suited to the air freight role, especially in view of the extensive night operations required by the industry, and its acquisition would allow TNT to enhance and expand even further its unique European express freight services. In fact, the 146-QT's exceptional

quietness soon led to reduced landing fees being offered by several airport authorities who were keen to attract the aircraft and the business it would bring.

G-TNTA was based at Prestwick Airport and TNT had its own in-house company, TNT International Aviation Services Ltd, charged with the purchase and management of its aircraft fleet. As an Australian company, TNT could not hold a UK Air Operator's Certificate, so its UK broker Air Foyle of Luton tendered successfully for the operation and crewing of the TNT 146s and a similar arrangement was followed with TNT 146 operators in Sweden, Italy, Spain and other European countries as the 146 fleet built up and new routes were added to the TNT network. BAe set up a small maintenance facility at Prestwick to support the TNT 146 operation, which now flew over a route from Prestwick to Belfast, Birmingham, Nuremburg, and Hannover, returning to Birmingham, Belfast and Prestwick; after returning to Birmingham from Germany, two Birmingham-Belfast sectors were flown before continuing on to Prestwick. The call at Dublin that used to be made on TNT-IPEC services was dropped due to Customs delays there, and all cargo for the Irish Republic now flies via Belfast, clearing Customs on the land border. G-TNTA's annual utilisation was initially around 2,500hr, and it was generally available for *ad hoc* charters during the daytime and at weekends.

The second 146-QT, G-TNTB, was delivered on 20 September 1987 and flew its first TNT service the next day in the hands of an Air Foyle crew; applications to the CAA for new route licences were not necessary as, technically, TNT was chartering the 146 from Air Foyle. The third 146-QT, G-BNPJ, was delivered to the Italian operator Mistral Air as I-TNTC on 3 December 1987, for services based on Rome's Ciampino Airport; Mistral Air was the first of the new European 146-QT operators to start under TNT's banner, and flew 146 services four nights a week linking Rome, Lyon and Milan to TNT's West German hubs of Hannover and Nuremburg, and also to Cologne.

TNT's big Commitment

Meanwhile, on 23 June 1987, just seven weeks after TNT had taken delivery of its first 146-QT G-TNTA, BAe announced a long-term commitment with the TNT Transport Group for the purchase of all the 146-QT freighters planned for production over the next five years, envisaged as a total of 72 aircraft in a programme valued at over US $1.5 billion. TNT was to acquire a substantial number of these for the planned expansion of its worldwide overnight freight service network, and by the end of 1989 firm orders had been placed for 23 146-QTs, including G-TNTA and the first two aircraft ordered soon after the latter's purchase. The balance of the 72 aircraft not needed by TNT were to be made available for onward sale or lease through Ansett Worldwide Aviation Services — AWAS, a subsidiary since 1986 of Ansett Transport Industries — ATI, of which the TNT Group is a co-owner. AWAS specialises in the leasing, sale and purchase of aircraft and related equipment and, with the resources of Ansett Airlines, it can offer operational and engineering support, as well as technical training and assistance. The agreement with TNT includes both the 146-200QT and the freighter version of the Series 300, the 146-300QT which became available late in 1989. TNT, through its close links with Ansett and its air freight operations, will be able to offer BAe considerable expertise and operational feedback in helping to develop future cargo and convertible passenger/cargo variants of the 146.

TNT's commitment to purchase most, if not all, of the 146-QTs built over the next five years represented one of the most important British civil aircraft orders for many years, rivalling in importance the Capital Airlines orders for Viscount 745s in 1954 and the American Airlines order for BAC One-Eleven 401s of 1963. It was unusual in that it did not specify an exact number of aircraft with options on a further number, but committed TNT in effect to almost as many 146-QTs as BAe could build. For this reason, and to meet likely future demand from other customers, a second 146 production line was set up at Woodford, near Manchester, to increase 146 production from 28 a year to 40 a year by 1990; four 146s were to be built here in 1988, the total building up progressively to 100 aircraft over a period of six years. As related in Chapter 6, the first Woodford-assembled 146 was Series 200, G-GRNZ, for Air Nova, which made its first flight as G-5-106 on 16 May 1988. At the same time as the TNT commitment, development was put in hand of a new quick-change convertible passenger/cargo variant of the 146 to be known as the 146QC.

Instead of ordering 146-QTs, TNT might theoretically have acquired some of the older Boeing 727-200s from its ATI subsidiary Ansett

Below:
The prototype 146-QT, now re-registered N146QT, with the 10ft 11in wide x 6ft 4in high cargo door open, and in a new colour scheme with dark blue, red and orange fuselage flashes.

Airlines and had them converted into freighters for its European routes. But this solution would have ignored not only the superior appeal of the 146-QT's quietness for night freighting but also the superior economics and long-term reliability of a new aircraft. As TNT Managing Director Neil Hansford explained: 'New aircraft are depreciated over a longer period than old aircraft, and when this is combined with a lower spares consumption and engineering costs, as well as better reliability, the operation of new aircraft is more economical.' Also, any prospective competitor of TNT's in Europe who might want to order 146-QTs would, because TNT have earmarked all production for the next five years, have to lease the aircraft from TNT's associate Ansett Worldwide Aviation Services, thus indirectly benefiting TNT itself.

TNT requested several special features for its 146s, reflecting the group's great experience in moving fast freight; these include additional wheel-brake temperature indicators, changes to allow flight up to 31,000ft to give access to Flight Level 280-320 Corridors (the 146's standard cruising height is 29,000ft) and installation of an improved Omega GNS/500A Series IV navigation system, to enable one particular sector time to be shortened by 12min. The 146-QT's despatch reliability has proved sufficiently good, at 99.5% after 12 months in service, for TNT to form TNT Overnight Air Express, which guarantees a next-day door-to-door delivery service.

By mid-1988, Air Foyle was flying the first two TNT 146-QTs over much the same UK-Germany route as a year before, but now including calls at Edinburgh and Luton as well as Cologne, and terminating every night at the Nuremburg hub; the call at Hannover was now dropped. After Mistral Air in Rome, the next European operator to start TNT 146 services was Malmo Aviation, which took delivery of 146-QT, SE-DEI (ex-G-BNUA), 11 February 1988 and with it

inaugurated a Stockholm-Gothenburg-Roskilde-Nuremburg route. The Swedish operator took delivery of a second 146, SE-DHM (ex-G-BOMJ), on 12 December 1988 (this is actually registered to Sandvik Leasing AB), and in May 1989 Malmo Aviation was bought by the Swedish leasing company Salenia Aviation. Salenia has two 146 Series 200s on order and is the parent company of Swedish commuter airline Salair, it also has a 25% holding in Air Bremen. The acquisition of Malmo Aviation, which also operates five Friendships, will help Salair exploit the under-utilised potential of its three Saab SF340QC commuter airliners. Salenia based a Malmo Aviation 146-QT at Stockholm's Bromma Airport late in 1990 in the livery of Salair.

The fifth 146-QT, G-BNYC, was at first earmarked for the French operator Euralair International as F-GTNT, but this registration was not taken up and instead it was re-registered G-TNTH for operation by Air Foyle, being delivered to them on 25 March 1988. Air Foyle leased it to Euralair for a year, from 11 April 1988 to 10 April 1989, for the operation of TNT flights from Paris, and on 2 June 1989 it was sold to a new Spanish freight charter operator Pan Air Lineas Aereas SA of Madrid, formed by Spanish private interests and with TNT holding a 25% stake. G-TNTH was allotted the provisional Spanish registration EC-281 on 2 June and became EC-EPA on 28 June. Pan Air started 146 operations for TNT in December 1988 with EC-ELT, which had left Hatfield on delivery to Spain on 24 October as EC-198; it had previously been G-BOKZ. Pan Air's 146s also fly *ad hoc* charters during the day and at weekends, as well as night freighting for TNT. A third 146-QT, G-BOMK, was at first earmarked for Pan Air as EC-231, but this was not taken up and instead it became first G-5-112 and then F-GTNU for Euralair, being delivered on 27 January 1989. Euralair took delivery of a second 146-QT, registered F-GTNT, on 10 May 1989; this was formerly G-BPBS and it is actually registered to the Orix Aircraft Corp of Japan, although operated by Euralair.

Meanwhile the sixth 146-QT, G-BOHK, was delivered to TNT Express (UK) Ltd as G-TNTJ on 30 September 1988 to be operated by Nürnberger Flugdienst GmbH — NFD, as D-ANTJ (in fact, the 100th 146 to be delivered). NFD was to start operations with the 146 in November 1988 and has discussed with BAe the possibility of a quick-change conversion of D-ANTJ for daytime passenger charters using palletised seating, but this idea has now been dropped. By this time Cologne had replaced Nuremberg as TNT's German hub, and the TNT Group had achieved a 1988 turnover of US $3.1 billion, making it the seventh largest freight/express distribution enterprise in the world. TNT also acquired XP Express Parcel Systems, which was a wholly-owned KLM subsidiary operating five Friendships and 11 light twins, and moved its operations from Maastricht in the Netherlands to its own hub at Cologne.

A joint express freight venture that could be a significant forerunner of things to come, following the sensational political changes in Eastern Europe in the last part of 1989, was made by TNT and the Hungarian state airline Malev, with Technoimpex, the Hungarian foreign trade organisation and Balbona, the country's state agricultural company, the forwarding agency Masped and the Magyar Hitel Bank also involved. This provides for the operation of 146-QT G-BOMI as HA-TAB on a five-nights-a-week freight service between Budapest and TNT's hub at Cologne; this 146 left Hatfield on delivery to Budapest on 18 November 1988, and is painted

in a joint TNT/Malev livery. During the day the 146 will be used on Malev's own freight network, replacing two Ilyushin Il-18 freighters on flights to other European destinations and also to North Africa. Malev also operates some 500 freight charter flights a year.

Hungary has embarked on a large-scale programme of privatisation of State industries, and is turning away from the rigid, over-centralised and excessively bureaucratic State control of Communist rule towards a market economy. The TNT/Malev operation could be the forerunner of others in Eastern Europe, and the 146-QT could play an important part in helping to rebuild the badly run-down economies of these countries after years of Communist rule.

At the 1988 SBAC Show at Farnborough, TNT had announced orders for 11 more 146s as part of its current total of 23 on order, and 10 of these were to be the 146-300QT freighter version of the Series 300. The first two of these, G-BRGK and G-BRGM, made their first flights on 16 August and 24 September 1989, and are going to Malmo Aviation as SE-DIM and SE-DIT respectively for use on behalf of TNT's newly acquired subsidiary XP Parcel Express Systems. SE-DIT was delivered first, on 13 February 1990, and will operate from Oslo to Gothenburg and Cologne. In Australia, TNT's associate Ansett Air Freight has taken delivery of two 146-200QTs for services on Australia's east coast, with VH-JJY (formerly G-BOXD) leaving Hatfield on 4 May 1989 for Australia, followed by VH-JJZ (ex-G-BOXE), which left on delivery on 3 June. Ansett New Zealand has leased from BAe the 146QC G-BPBT for a trial period; this left Woodford on its delivery flight on 4 October 1989, joining two 146 Series 200s in service with this operator and five Series 300s in the course of delivery. After only two months of its six months trial period, Ansett New Zealand bought the 146-QC G-BPBT outright; it was handed over to them at Norfolk Island on 24 January 1990, becoming ZK-NZC the following day. During its first full month of service with the airline the QC had flown 280 flights of an average 50 minutes duration, with a daily pattern of eight passenger sectors followed by two freight sectors, and the time to change from freight to passenger roles had averaged less than 30 minutes.

The Quick-Change 146

Development of a convertible quick-change passenger/cargo variant of the 146-200QT, able to switch rapidly from passengers by day to freight at night, by having the seats mounted on removable pallets, was put in hand when TNT announced its big commitment for up to 72 146-QTs, and details of the 146-QC quick-

change variant were announced at the 1989 Paris Salon Internationale. The first 146-QC, G-BPBT, was displayed statically at this event, later going to Ansett New Zealand on lease, and the QC programme was launched on the basis of 50 aircraft being sold by 1994. The QC conversion can be applied to both the Series 200 and 300, the cost of a 146-200QC being around US $23 million. This is bound to be more expensive than a standard passenger Series 200 because the QC variant has the freighter's reinforced floor and cargo door. The 146-200QC can carry six 108in x 88in pallets like the 146-QT freighter, or four 125in x 96in pallets, and in the passenger role can seat 85 people five-abreast at 31in pitch or 94 six-abreast. When converted for freight, passengers' overhead luggage bins, toilets and galleys are retained in the QC variant, the bins limiting pallet height and, with the toilets and galleys, slightly reducing the freight payload; the standard container used by TNT would have its top corners removed to clear the bins.

Although there is a slight loss of payload, the small express parcels that would be normal QC loads are carried more for their revenue value than volume. Conversion of a 146 from passenger to freight role can be completed in 30min, but one disadvantage of the QC concept, no matter what type of aircraft it is applied to, is potential deterioration to the interior caused by frequent changes from passenger-carrying to the freighting role. TNT is considering a larger galley and stowage area by the main door, catering for the business traveller, for any 146-QCs it may decide to operate, and the main cargo door would also be kept free of overhead luggage bins. The space for an extra half-pallet at the rear on the 146-QT freighter will be devoted to various galley options in the QC variant, and airstairs can be fitted. First customer for the 146-QC was the newly-formed Princess Air of Southend, which

Above:
Eight TNT Group 146-QTs, with the tail of a ninth just visible on the right, are pictured on the ground at their German base of Cologne. On the left is I-TNTC of Mistral Air behind SE-DHM of Malmo Aviation; in the centre are (from back to front) G-TNTB operated by Air Foyle, HA-TAB operated jointly by TNT and Hungary's state airline Malev, and F-GTNU of Euralair, while on the right are (from back to front) G-TNTJ (now D-ANTJ with Nürnberger Flugdienst), G-TNTH (now EC-EPA of Pan Air) and SE-DEI of Malmo Aviation. *Olivier Constant*

has ordered one, G-PRIN, plus one on option. Early in 1990 Princess Air confirmed its option for a second 146-QC, for delivery in April 1991, and pending delivery of the first QC has taken delivery of 146 Series 200 G-BRXT, named *Princess Alison*, and previously Air Nova's C-GRNY. This flew its first service on 6 April 1990 from Southend to Palma, Majorca, and back to Hurn airport, Bournemouth, making another flight from there to Palma and then back to Southend. The 146-QC G-PRIN began the first QC services in Europe with the type in July, flying up to 94 passengers by day on IT flights to the Channel Islands, Italy, Spain and Portugal, and carrying up to 9.5 tonnes of cargo from Southend to Cologne at night. A second 146-QC has now been ordered.

The Lyon-based French regional carrier Air Jet became the second European 146-QC customer in October when it ordered a single Series 200QC for delivery in September 1991. Air Jet was formed in May 1980 as part of the Jet Services group express parcel system and operates freight services from Paris-Orly to three other places using a trio of Fokker F27 Friendship 600QCs, a Beech Super King Air 200 and a Beech 90. It also flies passenger and freight services between Lyon and Avignon, and hopes to operate into London City airport with its 146.

Discussions with potential customers during recent sales and demonstration tours had convinced BAe by 1984 that a stretch of the 82-112 passenger Series 200 to seat 120-130 people would make good commercial sense. In March that year the new Fokker 100 — the Rolls-Royce Tay-powered successor to the F28 Fellowship — had been launched, and this 100-110 seater landed its first important order, from Swissair, in July 1984. This represented a clear threat to future 146 sales, and BAe announced preliminary details of the stretched 146, the 120-passenger Series 300, at the start of the 1984 SBAC Show at Farnborough. This was not, perhaps, the ideal time for BAe to contemplate the launching of a major new version of the 146, as earlier in the year it had had to fight a hard battle with the British government to secure adequate financial backing for its share of the A320 Airbus programme, the Government finally laying down fairly stringent conditions. There was also the cost of launching the ATP twin-turboprop successor to the 748, and the funding of BAe's share in the EAP fighter demonstrator, and BAe had also had to avert takeover bids from cash-rich electronic giants GEC and Thorne-EMI, although these were more interested in BAe's military business than its civil activities. But the possibility of a future takeover bid remained very much alive for a time.

In its original form, the 146 Series 300 fuselage was 10ft 11in longer than the Series

Below:
The first 146 Series 100, G-SSSH, in the course of conversion into the aerodynamic prototype Series 300, in which form it was re-registered G-LUXE.

200's, and maximum gross weight was increased by 10,500lb to 104,000lb. To cater for the increased weights, four uprated ALF 502R-7 turbofans would have been fitted of 7,500lb st (the ALF 502R-6 of the same thrust is also available for the Series 300). A new feature was the use of winglets, or wingtip fences, similar to those developed for the A310-300 Airbus to reduce induced drag. The flightdeck would have featured a new digital autopilot and revised avionics with either conventional instruments or an EFIS system with cathode ray tube displays, depending on the customer's choice. An EFIS flightdeck has been undergoing flight trials on BAe's 146 Series 300 G-OAJF, the first production 300, since 19 April 1989, and the EFIS cockpit is now certificated. By the end of 1990 twenty 146s with EFIS cockpits had been delivered to five operators. The 120-passenger Series 300 would generally, in its original form, have carried 20% more payload than the Series 200, but using only slightly more fuel. First flight of the Series 300 was planned for 1987, with deliveries starting early in 1988. Up to 130 passengers could be seated in a high-density interior, and the Series 300 was at first priced at US $18 million.

But, by 1986, airline market reaction to the Series 300 in its initial form had brought about some important changes. In particular the increase in fuselage length was now 15ft 9in, made up of a forward fuselage 'plug' of 8ft 1in and a rear fuselage 'plug' of 7ft 8in, these giving about 8ft more cabin length over the Series 200 and space for 15 more seats in five-abreast rows and also more cabin width. The extra cabin length is used for greater comfort rather than squeezing in as many passengers as possible

(up to 130 can be carried six-abreast), as it was now realised by BAe that comfort played a key role in the sale of short-haul jets, especially in the very important North American markets. With the tendency for regional airlines to operate as one of a group for a major domestic carrier under such banners as American Eagle or United Express, passengers transferring to a short-haul jet like the 146 from a 747 or DC-10 would continue to expect mainliner standards of comfort; six-abreast seating would no longer be attractive. Instead the revised Series 300 can carry 103 passengers five-abreast at 31in pitch in greatly increased comfort, with ample wardrobe and galley space.

Several other changes were made to the revised Series 300: the winglets at the wingtips were dispensed with, and powerplants reverted to the 6,970lb st ALF 502R-5 turbofans that already powered the Series 200 and 100, this change being made possible by a reduction in maximum take-off weight to 93,000lb from the 104,000lb originally proposed. Also dropped was the 'glass' EFIS flightdeck, largely to ensure commonality with existing 146 Series 200s with more conventional instrumentation for operators like Air Wisconsin, whose pilots would have had to obtain different type validation of licences to fly their Series 300s if these had been equipped with EFIS. Air Wisconsin had become the Series 300 launch customer in May 1987 when it changed five of an earlier order for Series 200s placed in September 1986, into 300s.

The prototype Series 100, G-SSSH, made its last flight in this form on 7 August 1986, as related in Chapter 3, and three days later went for conversion into the Series 300 aerodynamic prototype, its fuselage being lengthened by the insertion of two 'plugs'. It made its first flight in Series 300 form on 1 May 1987 with the new registration G-LUXE, and not long after was displayed at the 1987 Paris Salon Internationale. After completing its flight test programme, terminating in CAA certification in September 1988, it was retained for development work, and was rolled out at Hatfield on 30 May 1989 in full Ansett New Zealand livery, apparently for publicity purposes. The Series 300 offers similar seating capacities at five-abreast as the Series 200 does at six-abreast, while retaining the good field performance and exceptional quietness of the early models; by comparison, the Fokker 100 has five-abreast seating for up to 107 in a smaller fuselage cross-section. A typical high-density interior for the Series 300 would seat 112 passengers, but when Type III emergency exits are installed in the centre, this can be increased to 128 passengers six-abreast at 29in pitch.

Earlier in its career, the 146 came in for some criticism from several operators regarding the amount of aerodynamic noise inside the passenger cabin. In the Series 300 this problem has been solved by engineering carried out on the wing root fillets, flap tracks and door seals to

reduce internal noise levels, as well as by silencing a hydraulic pump. Cabin sidewalls for the Series 300 have been designed to offer an extra 2in space at shoulder level and there are capacious new lockers for overhead hand luggage. There is also a wardrobe unit at the front of the cabin on the starboard side, and extra galley space with units at both ends of the cabin.

The Series 300 was originally cleared for a maximum take-off weight of 93,000lb, but a minor thickening of wing skins allows this weight to be increased to 95,000lb for the first few Series 300s, the maximum landing weight being 83,000lb and maximum zero-fuel weight 77,500lb. As well as the two fuselage 'plugs', structural alterations that distinguish the Series 300 include strengthened fuselage keel panels, a thicker top skin and material changes to the wing, and the strengthening of the fuselage centre section. Some of these alterations, such as the strengthened centre section, will be standard for later production Series 100s, giving this variant an increase in maximum take-off weight that can be converted into an extra 400 miles of range.

The 300's extra length gives it a total under-floor freight hold capacity of 812cu ft. The 146-300QT freighter can carry a payload of up to 27,535lb in seven standard 108in x 88in pallets, and for the quick-change 300QC payload is 23,774lb. Design studies have been carried out of several stretched freighter variants to carry higher volumetric loads. Among these was the Series 350, a development of the 300 with the fuselage lengthened by inserting another 'plug' of about 5ft to allow eight or nine standard pallets to be carried.

First Deliveries

The first of five Series 300s for Air Wisconsin was N611AW, which had first flown as G-BOWW on 30 August 1988. This became G-5-0120 and then N146UK before leaving Hatfield on 12 November on a demonstration tour of the States prior to delivery to Air Wisconsin on 16 December; it became N611AW the following June. It was followed by N612AW, which left Hatfield on delivery on 23 December 1988, N614AW on 24 May 1989, N615AW on 9 September and N616AW which left Hatfield for Air Wisconsin on 4 November. Next customer was Air UK Ltd, which ordered two Series 300s for the former British Caledonian routes from London-Gatwick to Edinburgh and Glasgow that it had taken over in October 1988. The first of these, G-UKHP, was delivered on 28 February 1989 and was followed by G-UKSC on 10 March, both of which have accommodation for 110 passengers. The first one flew its first service from Gatwick to Edinburgh and Glasgow on 2 March. A repeat order for four more 300s was placed, the first of these, G-UKAC, being delivered to Air UK on 20 November 1989, and these will supplement the airline's four Series 200s. Dan-Air took delivery of a single Series 300, G-BPNT, on 2 June 1989 to supplement its three Series 100s; this flew its first service, from London-Gatwick to Belfast, on 6 June.

At the end of 1988, Thai Airways International ordered two Series 300s for domestic and regional routes, followed by two more the following April. The first pair, HS-TBK named *Chiang Kham* and HS-TBL named *Sukhirim*, left Woodford on delivery to Bangkok on 28 April and 23 June 1989 respectively, HS-TBL having previously been registered as G-BRAB to BAe for display at the 1989 Paris Salon Internationale. Of the second pair HS-TBM — *Watthana Nakom*, and HS-TBN — the first left Woodford on delivery on 22 November, and by this time the 300s were achieving 99.3% on-time departures — the highest technical despatch reliability in Thai Airways' fleet. The airline also uses Series 100, HS-TBO, from airfields with shorter runways. Thai Airways has expressed a desire for more power for its Series 300s on the grounds that this variant cannot lift a full load out of high short airstrips at temperatures above ISA + 15°C. The airline may change its 300s, which are at present leased on a monthly rental basis from BAe, for several Series 100s.

The first two of five Series 300s for Ansett New Zealand, ZK-NZF and ZK-NZG, both left Hatfield on delivery on 9 December 1989, to be followed shortly after by ZK-NZH, ZK-NZI and ZK-NZJ. As related in Chapter 5, these supplement two Series 200s on domestic routes linking Auckland, Wellington, Christchurch, Dunedin, Rotorua, Mount Cook and Queenstown. The 300s seat 90 passengers and these 146s represent a NZ$280 million re-equipment programme for Ansett New Zealand, which was formed on 13 February 1985 as Newmans Air, with Ansett Transport Industries of Australia acquiring a 50% holding in 1986. The other shareholders are Brierley Investments (27.5%) and the Newmans Group (22.5%).

Another Ansett group operator, East-West Airlines of New South Wales, announced an order for eight Series 300s plus four on option in September 1989 for delivery, beginning in the summer of 1990. East-West operates services from Sydney to destinations in New South Wales, Victoria, Tasmania, Queensland and the Northern Territory, as well as to Canberra and to Norfolk Island in the Pacific. East-West was for many years the only private airline (except for commuter operators) outside the Ansett orbit, but

Below:
Air Wisconsin was the first Series 300 customer with an order for five and the first of these, to become N611AW, is seen in United Express livery in the static park at Farnborough 1988 with the British registration G-BOWW.
M. J. Hardy

in 1987 it was acquired by the TNT Transport Group and News Corp, the co-owners of Ansett Transport Industries. The new Hawaiian carrier Discovery Airways has seven Series 300s on order, plus two on option, and is in the process of taking delivery of five Series 200s. A recent 300 customer is the Italian operator AeroTaxi Sud, a subsidiary of an Italian industrial group, which has ordered two for delivery in June and July 1990 for use on high-quality inclusive tours from Naples, Rome and Milan. Shortly after placing this order this operator changed its name to Sagittair and took delivery of its first Series 300, I-ATSC, on 21 June; this was fitted with a 100-seat five-abreast interior and began operating IT flights to destinations including Portugal, Greece and Egypt. The second Series 300, I-ATSD, was delivered on 10 July. One of the latest 300 customers is Makung Airlines of Taiwan (or Formosa), which ordered two 112-seater Series 300s with options on two more for delivery in July and December 1990 to cater for increasing traffic on the Taipei-Kaohsiung and Taipei-Makung domestic routes. Makung Airlines, which had earlier bought the last two BAe 748s from the Woodford production line, has specified the recently-introduced Type III mid-cabin emergency exits for its Series 300s, which will allow passenger seating to be increased to 122. Makung's first Series 300 appeared with the Formosan registration B-1775 but was actually delivered on 3 August 1990 with the British registration G-BSOC, flying its first service on 2 September.

In Australia East-West Airlines (now known as Eastwest Airlines), began services, concentrating very much on the leisure destinations, with its first two of eight 96-passenger Series 300s, VH-EWI and VH-EWJ, in the first week of September 1990; these had both left Hatfield on their delivery flights on 25 August. Among the firm orders for 25 aircraft announced on the eve of Farnborough 1990 was a second Series 300 for Dan-Air Services, and Air UK took up a previously announced option for two Series 300s. Dan-Air's second 300, G-BTNU, had already been delivered when the order was announced, and flew its first service, from Gatwick to Jersey and return, on 21 August. A repeat order from Thai Airways International for five Series 300s worth $100 million was among the 25 new orders revealed, and deliveries of these were to have begun in May 1991. They will continue as the lease on each of Thai's current 146s (which are leased from BAe for a monthly rental of $200,000 per aircraft) expires. The Series 200s may be returned to BAe when the new 300s are delivered, or retained in service if traffic growth warrants it. Altogether 48 Series 300s have been ordered up to October 1990, plus four on option, as well as 10 146-300QT freighters. Development of the Series 300 has probably cost around £75 million, not all of which has been paid by BAe.

Future Prospects

A re-engined 146 has been studied, and one possible powerplant was the new Rolls-Royce RB580 turbofan of 6,500-7,100lb take-off thrust, with a growth potential to around 10,000lb st. This was being studied jointly with Allison, and featured a quiet, efficient wide-chord fan based on RB211 design and a low-pressure turbine based on RB211 and Tay technology, combined with a high-efficiency compressor, low-emission combustors and a high-pressure turbine from the Allison T406 turboshaft engine that powers the Bell/Boeing tilt-rotor V-22 Osprey.

However, early in 1990 Rolls-Royce pulled out of joint development of the RB580 with Allison because the British firm felt its priorities to be with big fan engines like the RB211 Trent. Allison is continuing to develop the basic RB580 as the GMA 3007 for Brazil's 50-seater Embraer EMB-145 regional jet.

In place of the RB580 for future 146 variants, Textron Lycoming is developing a new variant of the existing ALF 502 turbofan for a range of future new 146 versions; this was at first known as the ALF 502R-6 but is now redesignated the LF507, being the first member of the new LF500 family of turbofans. The LF507 is to power every variant of the 146 from its first delivery to BAe in the third quarter of 1991, including the RJ70 and RJ80 regional jet versions, as well as several new models of the 146 itself. The LF507 differs chiefly from the ALF 502R-5 in having another stage added to its low pressure compressor to increase the thrust rating to about 7,200lb, or over 200lb st more than the present ALF 502R-5. This, say the manufacturers, will improve 'hot and high' performance and second-stage climb, and the LF507 will develop 7,000lb thrust at 23.3°C (ISA + 8.3°C) whereas the existing R-5 develops the same thrust at 15°C. Turbine gas temperatures (TGT) of the new LF507 are also significantly lower, by about 100°, with more than twice the margin below the TGT limit now available at take-off compared to the ALF 502R-5. This is especially important as higher fuel prices (made worse by the Gulf crisis in early 1991) are causing prospective customers to look more carefully at fuel burn per seat.

The LF507 will make possible performance improvements across the entire range, and an increase in design weight for all 146 versions, as well as in payload and range. Full authority digital

engine control (FADEC) will give cooler starting and optimised control for the LF507. Another advantage of the new engine will be its relatively low carbon and nitrogen emissions, which are now a factor in the determination of landing fees by some airport authorities.

BAe has also studied the unducted fan — or propfan-type of powerplant for the 146, and a design study of a 146 powered by two advanced propfans was shown in model form on the BAe stand at the 1986 Farnborough show. These propfans were not pylon-mounted but underslung from the wing, making for a higher thrust line, and they featured long streamlined spinners. The ALF 502 has given good service and unexcelled quietness in operation; by 1989 a total of 2,200,000hr had been flown in BAe 146s by 505 of these engines. Following the discovery of cracks in the ALF 502's high-pressure compressor discs, both the CAA and the American FAA issued a Mandatory Airworthiness Directive in the summer of 1989 requiring the checking of engines after a certain number of flights. Those 146s which have completed 12,000 or more flights must undergo inspection of their discs within the next 250 flights, or within the next 100 for aircraft that have flown 14,000 or more flights.

These cracks were first noticed during routine engine inspections at USAir, and were the subject of a Textron Service Bulletin in January 1989. A new coating process has been incorporated into disc manufacture to cure this problem. BAe has selected Smiths Industries primary engine displays for installation on all future production 146s, the first installations commencing in March 1990. BAe placed an initial order for 40 sets of these displays, worth over £2 million, in 1989, and similar displays have been selected as a basic fit for the 737-300, -400 and -500 and the McDonnell Douglas MD-80 series.

The RJ70

A new variant of the 146 known as the RJ70 (for Regional Jet 70-seater) was unveiled at the June 1990 meeting of the Regional Airlines Association in Washington, DC. This was not an outright launch but rather a 'testing of the water' to gauge airline customer reaction, especially among the US regionals, to the idea of a four-engined 70-seater regional jet. The RJ70 is to be based on the 146 Series 100 airframe with current 146 systems, including an EFIS flightdeck, and four de-rated Textron Lycoming LF507 turbofans; the exact amount by which the LF507 will be de-rated has yet to be decided, but will be about 10% down on the existing engines, giving a thrust of about 6,100 to 6,250lb st.

The RJ70 is aimed mainly at the now buoyant US regional airline market and would be built on the existing 146 production line at Woodford with a first flight likely in the second quarter of 1991. BAe hopes it will have a common pilot rating with the 146, and is setting the RJ70's flyaway price at $18 million, or some $2 million more than that of the smaller 50-seat Canadair RJ regional jet, for which orders and options for 139 aircraft are held, and Embraer's 50-seat EMB-145 Amazon turbofan-powered derivative of the EMB-120 Brasilia. BAe claims that the RJ70 will break even with a 30-passenger load over a 300nm sector — admittedly two

or three more passengers than competing types — but for this, the operator gets a lot more aircraft. Commonality with existing 146 fleets is an obvious sales point, and BAe's studies have found strong interest in the 50-70 passenger range. An initial market for as many as 400 to 600 airliners in the 50-80 seater category is foreseen.

While the RJ70 with five-abreast seating is aimed at the US regional markets, the RJ80, with six-abreast seating for 80 passengers, which was first revealed two months after the RJ70, is aimed at the European markets and at customers in the rest of the world outside the USA. Like the RJ70, the RJ80 is based on the Series 100 airframe and will be powered by de-rated LF507 turbofans. The new engine is now being flight-tested on a Series 300 demonstrator, and in October and November 1990 BAe took what it calls 'a representative RJ70' with a 70-seat interior and gated engines to simulate the de-rated LF507s on a sales tour of the Americas, which included a visit to the Regional Airlines Association meeting in November at Phoenix, Arizona. QC — or Quick-Change — versions of both the RJ70 and RJ80 will be offered in due course, and new mid-cabin exits now allow a Combi configuration for all QC variants in which both passengers and freight containers can be carried together.

Also featured on the RJ70 and RJ80 are 'Phase II' avionics capable of Category IIIA operations down to 200m horizontal visibility and 50ft decision height, autothrottle, digital flight guidance system and a digital inertial reference system. A revised Honeywell-Sperry EFIS system is also incorporated with a new integrated windshear warning system, a digital radio altimeter and radio/navigation systems. A traffic alert and collision avoidance system will be offered as an optional 'extra'. Present 146 versions are already being offered with a 'glass cockpit' based around an EFIS digital display of analogue-derived flight data as part of the Phase I avionics update, and the Phase II avionics fit would be available to 146 customers from the third quarter of 1992.

The RJ80 will be what is termed a 'baseline passenger' airliner with larger carry-on baggage space and less sophisticated galleys. The RJ80's basic price, like that of the RJ70, is being set at $18 million, which compares to $21 million for a Series 100, $21.5 million for a Series 200 and $22.5 million for a Series 300. The new LF507 engines and the latest avionics fit could add up to $750,000 to each model's price. BAe reports strong airline interest in the new RJ70 and RJ80 from operators in South America and Canada, with Varig of Brazil tipped as a likely customer; other sales targets are Air Canada Connector airlines like Air BC and Air Nova, and Canadian Partner airlines like Air Atlantic. Airlines that have ordered the Canadair RJ regional jet will be prime targets for BAe's RJ70 and RJ80 sales teams, and among the sales points they will be stressing is that the RJ70 and RJ80 cabin is of proper airliner size, whereas that of the Canadair RJ is much smaller, being based on that of the Challenger executive jet.

Other new 146 variants to be powered by LF507 turbofans are a QC version of the Series 100 that will be able to carry up to 79 passengers or five freight containers, and a freighter version, the Series 100QT. The LF507's

extra thrust will make possible an increase in design weights for the Series 100, 200 and 300 by wing, fuselage and undercarriage strengthening, and the extra power and higher weights will lead to improved airfield performance and give up to double the range from limited runways. The LF507 will make possible payload increases of up to 28% on the 146 Series 100,13% on the Series 200 and 12% on the Series 300. For the other QC variants, payload increases made possible by the LF507s are 16% passengers and 13% freight for the Series 200QC, and 15% passengers and 12% freight for the 300QC. The 200QC can now seat up to 97 passengers and the 300QC up to 106.

The Twin-Engined 146-NRA

In November 1990 both Fokker and Deutsche Aerospace — DASA announced independently their separate intentions of building a 130-seater regional jet airliner to capture a slice of a market for 70- to 130-seater regional jets estimated at 4,000 to 5,000 aircraft in the next 25 years. Preliminary details were released of the Fokker 130, a stretched derivative of the Fokker 100 with a fuselage about 18ft longer, increased wing span and a target delivery date of 1996. DASA, which already has a 27% share in Fokker 100 production, might have seemed a logical partner for this project but instead is to design and build its own 80- to 130-seater from scratch, preferably within a European partnership. DASA had in fact had discussions with BAe over joint development of a regional jet early in 1990 but these talks foundered over DASA's insistence on leading the programme. Talks were also held with Aerospatiale of France and Aeritalia of Italy (who together make ATR 42 and 72 regional turboprops), and with CASA of Spain.

These talks bore fruit in March 1991 with an agreement signed between DASA, Aerospatiale and Alenia (the recently merged Aeritalia/Selenia

group) for the launch of an 80-130 seater regional jet, expected during the third quarter of 1991; this would first fly in 80-90 seater form in 1996, with entry into airline service two years later, with a 130-seater version following two years after that. DASA claimed that Government support for the $2.5 billion programme was almost certain, and with continuing sales of the ATR 42 and 72, and Aerospatiale negotiating with Boeing for the purchase (now agreed) of de Havilland Canada, makers of the DHC-7 Dash Seven and DHC-8 Dash Eight regional turboprops, BAe had to come up with a 130-seater development of the 146 to meet the challenge of the Fokker 130 and the new DASA jet.

BAe's answer to this requirement is the 146-NRA (these letters stand for New Regional Aircraft) with twin engines, an entirely new wing and a fuselage stretched by 18ft to seat up to 139 passengers in a six-abreast interior or 125 passengers five-abreast in a single-class layout; various mixed-class seating arrangements can be specified, and a new flight deck is featured. The fuselage stretch would be equivalent to about five seat rows, and would consist of a 'plug' forward and aft of the wing. An entirely new wing of 11ft greater span than the 86ft 0in span of the existing 146 wing will be featured, and would have winglets on the tips but — like the existing wing — would avoid the complication of leading edge devices such as flaps. The new wing would have a much higher aspect ratio to give a design cruising speed of Mach 0.82 at 39,000ft. Wing plan form will be slightly different, with more sweep on the leading edge, and there are likely to be skin thickness changes as part of a general beefing up of the structure to take a higher gross weight.

The new wing is made necessary by two much more powerful engines of around 22,000lb st each chosen for their commonality with those of bigger airliners, and at the time of writing the most likely choices are the CFM International CFM56-3 as used in the Boeing 737-300 and '-500, or a derated variant of the IAE V2500, while talks are continuing with Rolls-Royce on the proposed Tay 690 intended to power the Fokker 130. Another possible powerplant is one of the BMW/Rolls-Royce BR700 family of engines designed especially for the new generation of regional jet airliners, while the new SNECMA M123 engine based on the military M88 turbofan is another possibility, as are two new versions of the CFM56 proposed, the CFM56-5C4 and CFM56-5C5; SNECMA and General Electric are partners in CFM International, who make the CFM56. The new 146-NRA wing will give sufficient ground clearance to instal even larger diameter ultra high by-pass ratio turbofans when they become available.

The 146-NRA is being proposed in two basic variants, a basic one with a maximum take-off weight of 118,200lb and a long range variant with increased fuel tankage and a maximum take-off weight of 124,052lb, which would have a range of 2,600 miles in 125-passenger form. BAe is actively seeking a minimum of two risk-sharing partners to collaborate on the 146-NRA project, which is likely to cost around $1 billion to develop, and it is hoped to launch the 146-NRA formally in 1991 with an in-service target date of 1996. From the start the wisdom of having two 130-seater European regional jet projects, by Fokker and DASA, was questioned and it seems unlikely that there will be room for all three. The 146-NRA, like the other two, appears at a bad

Below:
The prototype 146 Series 300, G-LUXE, in the livery of Ansett New Zealand, which operates five 90-passenger Series 300s on domestic routes linking cities in New Zealand's North and South Islands. *J. M. G. Gradidge*

time for the travel trade, when airlines are still feeling the effects of recession and the Gulf war on their traffic, and BAe itself has had to make job cutbacks and has yet to recover the development costs of the RJ70 and RJ80 from orders.

By October 1990, orders and options for the 146 totalled 294 aircraft, made up as follows: 37 Series 100s, 116 Series 200s plus 16 on option, 15 146 200QTs, four Series 200QCs, 48 Series 300s plus four on option (some other options may be for either 200s or 300s), and 10 146-300QT freighters. In addition there is the TNT commitment for 72 freighters, of which it has so far ordered 23, which are included in the above totals. Firm orders had yet to be placed for the RJ70 and RJ80 at the time of writing. By the end of May 1990, 146s all over the world had completed a total of one million flights, and were then serving with 38 operators worldwide; major airlines were then averaging 275 one-hour flights per month with a despatch reliability exceeding 98.5%. Of the 147 aircraft delivered by then, a total of 124 had been exported — or 84%.

This order book may seem modest by the standards of the Boeing 737 or the MD-80 series, but the 146 was the first major British airliner to sell without the benefit of any order from the State airline, as well as the first to have American instead of British engines. It was launched at a time when the economic storm clouds were gathering, and it might easily have suffered the fate of so many other British aircraft projects and been cancelled, but it survived a worldwide recession to be relaunched successfully. It may seem a modest, technically undemanding sort of aeroplane to serve as the civil flagship of an industry that produced such technically advanced airliners as the Viscount, Comet and Britannia, but the 146's claim to be the world's quietest jetliner accords perfectly with today's concern for the environment and the quality of life.

Tails of the fourth 146 Series 100, G-OBAF (ex-G-SCHH), in British Air Ferries livery; the third Series 100, G-SSCH, in Dan-Air colours; and the first Series 200, G-WISC, in Air Wisconsin livery at the 1982 Farnborough display, with an Airbus A310-220 in the background. Saab-Scania of Sweden builds the 146's tailplane, elevators and rudder.